COUNSELING
THROUGH
SCRIPTURE
NEW TESTAMENT

THE ASSOCIATION OF BIBLICAL COUNSELORS
General Editor SHAUNA VAN DYKE

COUNSELING THROUGH SCRIPTURE NEW TESTAMENT

THE ASSOCIATION OF BIBLICAL COUNSELORS

ISBN 978-1-7344406-3-8

TABLE OF CONTENTS

TABLE OF
CONTENTS (cont)

TABLE OF
CONTENTS (cont)

> **"**God gave us the Bible not just to inform our minds, but also to transform our hearts.**"**
> – John Piper

The Bible is the authoritative Word of God, so the life-giving truths we find in Scripture is sufficient for all matters of life and contains all that we need in order to know God's will and live a life pleasing to Him.

> *All Scripture is breathed out by God and profitable for teaching, for reproof, for correction, and for training in righteousness, that the man of God may be competent, equipped for every good work* (2 Timothy 3:16–17).

In your call to counsel, the Bible equips us for good works and gives us practical principles to help others live out in obedience to God. As we encourage others to surrender and submit to Scripture it will transform their hearts, which allows them to grow in spiritual maturity. My prayer is that this book will offer a simple and efficient way to gain understanding of God's Word, strengthen the way you counsel and equip you to speak the truth in love. May you be blessed as you walk others through the New Testament Scriptures, ministering in the relatable and raw moments of their story.

I am incredibly grateful the Lord gave me this assignment and for the support of my brothers and sisters in Christ. It is a privilege to work alongside so many gifted teachers and counselors. My prayer is we will later expand this book while also creating additional resources using other books of the Bible. A huge thank you to all my friends in ministry who participated in this project and to the ABC team for your continued support.

To the Glory of God Alone,

Shauna Van Dyke

MATTHEW 5 *2-12*

BLESSED AMID OUR SUFFERING

By: Darby Strickland
www.ccef.org

Backstory for Counselor: The gospel of Matthew begins and ends with the notion that Jesus is the King. The King has come and his kingdom is near. Jesus announces the presence of his kingdom by doing miracles and healing people. Each miracle in Matthew is a little glimpse of what the new kingdom will be like, where people are being restored, diseases healed, and evil spirits banished. The Sermon on the Mount is about what it is like for us to live as citizens in this new kingdom. We were born into a troubled kingdom of darkness and trouble, but in this new kingdom of light, Jesus will redeem broken and bruised lives. The Sermon on the Mount is very counter-cultural but beautifully transformative. It promises that Jesus brings fulfillment (Matt 5:17–18).

The Beatitudes are well known but often misunderstood as a way to live better or a list of things to aspire to be. But these are not things that we can do on our own. His kingdom comes to us; by God's grace it is gifted. Jesus is talking about a deep transformation that permeates our hearts, one that he accomplishes for us. It is not within our own strength to live this out; in fact, the Beatitudes invite us to say, "Lord help me, I cannot live this way." (emphasis added) In fact, much of the rest of the Sermon on the Mount rips away from us the self-delusion that we are capable of acquiring a state of blessedness on our own. It aims to produce in us a genuine poverty of spirit. We learn that we don't have the spiritual resources in ourselves to put Jesus' teachings into practice. We can't fulfill God's call by ourselves. For those suffering, our goal here is to highlight the great comfort in this truth.

Truth for Counselee: Each of the first four of the Beatitudes names a group of people we would normally regard as afflicted—the poor, mourners, meek, and hungry. These are not things that in this world we would aspire to be. Great suffering can have these impacts upon people: it strips us bare in ways that our vulnerability is almost too much to bear. This passage challenges us to think about how our vulnerabilities leave us in need of God. But what is life-giving is that Jesus is promising that he has blessed the vulnerable by granting them a relationship with the Lord and he promises to deliver us from our bondage. It is not that the vulnerable person must be better or have more faith, but that God has by His grace already blessed us in these ways. Jesus is simply declaring how blessed they are.

IN SESSION COUNSELING

Read Matthew 5:2–12 aloud and discuss the following three questions.
- What do you think Jesus is wanting his people to hear? *Or* who is on Jesus' heart as he is speaking?
- Why might Jesus have started with the "*blessed be poor in spirit*" or we might rephrase it as "blessed are those who know their need of God's grace"?
- Which of the attributes feel like they fit your situation?

What does this passage show us about Jesus?
- What does Jesus value?
- When you think about what you know about Jesus life and death, how do these Beatitudes describe him?
- Suffering often surprises us or challenges our faith. How might we think differently about our suffering if we were to expect that what happened to Jesus will also happen to us?

The Beatitudes are things that Jesus proclaims to be true about himself, but also about his people.
We have often thought that we have to do better, and other people might even tell us that we should be "suffering better." If we do not understand Jesus' heart for his people we might misread this passage as saying, these things *should be your attitudes*! But that is not the thrust of this passage. These are things that Jesus proclaims to be already true of his people, based on how he relates to us.

- If we think about the Beatitudes as promises made to you, what strikes you?
- What are the citizens of his kingdom like? There is a reversal as to what our culture values, what contrasts do you see?
- CENTRAL POINT: We often think of great suffering as misshaping us. The vulnerability and brokenness that come with great suffering can feel overwhelming. Let the Beatitudes challenge you here. How might your vulnerabilities, wounds, hurts, and brokenness be beautiful in Christ's Kingdom?

How has your heart responded to your suffering? (*key place to park with counselee*)
- What are ways you have suffered as a citizen of the Lord's kingdom? (As a counselor you might point this out as an encouragement.)
    - How has your suffering highlighted your faith?
    - God's faithfulness to you?
- What are the ways you have suffered as a citizen of this world? (Not living with these promises in mind)
    - Where have you struggled with how suffering has shaped you?
    - Are there ways your suffering caused you to question the Lord's care of you?

AFTER SESSION ASSIGNMENT

After hearing from your particular counselee, choose one of the most fitting Beatitudes for them to mediate and journal on. For some, the exercise would build on where they already are making encouraging connections. For others, the assignment might be used to refocus their hearts to give them a new truth to dwell on.

[3] **"Blessed are the poor in spirit, for theirs is the kingdom of heaven."**
Jesus is declaring that those who recognize our desperate need of him are blessed. We do not have it within ourselves, to be redeemed or to be restored or to live as he calls

us to. So, we gratefully can turn to Jesus who does not just help us but also delights in extending God's grace. He promises the kingdom of heaven to those who know that they are spiritually needy.

* In your season of suffering, how is this freeing?
* How does this help you be honest about your struggles and doubts?
* Can you pray or write to the Lord about how this suffering has left you depleted and empty, asking for his help?

4 "Blessed are those who mourn, for they shall be comforted."
When we face evil or loss our response is sorrow. Being grieved deeply by the brokenness of the world is a right response. Sometimes we mourn the loss of people, other times we mourn the effects of evil that has happened to us, the fallen nature of this world, and our own hearts. God says he sees our sorrow and comforts us.

* How has the Lord comforted you?
* If your experience is more like the Psalmist (Psalm 22) who wonders where the Lord is, how can you lament this asking while asking for the comfort he promises?
* What are ways you see Jesus mourning in Scripture? (Matt 14:13; John 11:33–35; Luke 19:41; Hebrews 4:15; 5:7–9)

5 "Blessed are the meek, for they shall inherit the earth."
We wrongly assume that meekness means weakness or timidity. But the biblical understanding of meekness is power under control. Moses was described as the meekest man on earth (Num 12:3). Jesus describes himself as "meek and lowly" (Matt 11:28–29). Meek people are not prideful nor do they serve themselves. Rather they understand, as Christ and Moses did, that they are servants of God. Flowing from the second beatitude we have sorrow over the brokenness in our hearts and in this world. This meekness helps us not to seek our own justice, but be a servant of the just king who promises that we will inherit the earth.

* How has our culture encouraged us to seek our own justice? Has that tempted you to be aggressive in seeking justice for what has happened to you? Or fed unrighteous anger?
* God is just and he promises justice. He sees and knows how you were harmed. We are still called to seek justice, but with a heart that looks like Christ's, "but to do justice, and to love kindness, and to walk humbly with your God" (Micah 6:8). How can this help shape your response?
* What does it mean to you in this hard season to know that you will inherit the earth? What will the waiting be like for you?

⁶ **"Blessed are those who hunger and thirst for righteousness, for they shall be satisfied."**

When Jesus spoke about the righteous, he was talking about those who sought to have right relationships—with God and with the people around them. Right relationships flow from meekness (the third beatitude) because we can only form right relationships when we are emptied of ourselves and seek to serve the Lord and others. If we know we have God's grace for this, we will hunger and thirst for a right relationship with the Lord. and with the people around us (Matt 7:15–20. We cannot do this in our own strength, but only in recognition of our own emptiness, mourning our own unrighteousness, by submitting to God. Peace with people while on earth is not always possible, butGod promises to satisfy our longings.

- How have deep seasons of suffering strained your relationship with the Lord?
- Have you found a way to speak to the Lord about your distress about this?
- Jesus too was hurt by those he loved. How did his relationship with his father sustain him? (Matt 26: 36–56)
- If your suffering has caused broken relationships, journal about what that has been like.

"Righteousness has several senses in Scripture. Paul emphasized the legal righteousness that we receive through the atoning work of Christ. That is certainly present in Matthew. He calls Jesus a "ransom for many" (20:28) and he describes the atonement itself (27:38–46). But in Matthew 5, Jesus primarily describes the personal righteousness of disciples, who put aside murder, anger, and adultery. They give to oppressors and love their enemies (vv. 22–48). Thirsty disciples also pursue the mercy, purity, and peacemaking of the next few beatitudes (vv. 7–9)." Doriani, D. Blessed are those who hunger and thirst for righteousness by Dan Doriani. Ligonier Ministries. Retrieved January 12, 2022, from:
https://www.ligonier.org/learn/articles/blessed-are-those-who-hunger-and-thirst-for-righteousness

NOTES

MATTHEW 16
21-23

DISCERNING DAILY SPIRITUAL WARFARE

By: Shannon Kay McCoy

www.shannonkaymccoy.com

In Matthew 16, Jesus openly announced His coming suffering, death, and resurrection. Displeased with this information, Peter pulled Jesus aside and rebuked Him. Then Jesus came back with a rebuke. This story reveals how we are fighting a real spiritual battle. If we ignore it, then we can become mouthpieces for Satan. This Bible narrative is crucial for believers to understand how to discern spiritual warfare in our daily lives.

IN SESSION COUNSELING
Read Matthew 16:21–23 and discuss the following points.

What was the momentous message Jesus was teaching his disciples in v. 21?
- Jesus was preparing them for imminent events.
- Jesus predicted that he would be killed and on the third day be raised. His suffering, death, and resurrection are necessary in the salvation plan of God. Peter was to learn that suffering and glory always go together.
- Have you received this truth into your heart?

Why did Peter rebuke Jesus in v. 22?
- After hearing what Jesus said, the outspoken disciple, Peter, vehemently disapproved the message because he feared Jesus being killed and implications of his death for the Jews.
- Jesus' message did not line up with Peter's expectation of Jesus' kingship on earth. He did not fully understand Jesus' mission on earth.
- In Matthew 16:16 Peter professed the deity of Christ and Jesus commended him. How could Peter in his next breath rebuke Jesus to his face?
- How do you respond when life does not go as you expected? Have you ever protested God's will and way in your life?

Why did Jesus respond with a rebuke toward Peter in v. 23?
- Jesus's response revealed that Peter became a mouthpiece for Satan when he rejected God's path for Jesus. Peter was expressing the desire of Satan, to keep Jesus from his work of redemptive suffering on the cross.
- Satan was using Peter to be a stumbling block in Christ's path of obedience.
- Peter's desires were not set on the things of God but on the things of man.
- Have you been a mouthpiece for Satan when you resisted the things of God for your desires and expectations?
- In the book of Job, God showed us how Satan intervenes in our lives. How might/ does the conflict between God and Satan express itself in your life? (Job 1:21; 2:10)

AFTER SESSION ASSIGNMENT

1. Peter was a strong believer but was wrong. What did you learn about discerning spiritual warfare in your daily life? How do you respond when life does not go as you planned? Will you seek your will that makes you susceptible to Satan's way or will you accept God's will?

2. Read Ephesians 6:10–20 List the weapons of warfare that we have in Christ. How can you use the armor of God daily to discern spiritual warfare in your life?

3. Read Colossians 2:15; Hebrews 2:14–15; and 1 John 3:8–12. Christ defeated Satan at the cross. What do these passages teach about what happens to Satan and what happens to believers?

MATTHEW 21
28-32

DISCERNMENT IN PARENTING

By: Jay Younts
www.everydaytalk247

Parents come to counseling wanting help in how to respond to their teenage son who is often slow to obey and frequently challenges requests or direction to do a particular task. They are convinced their son is rebellious at heart. After discussing relevant history with the parents, you discover that their son typically does accomplish what he was asked, even if he is not happy about it. This New Testament parable provides insight for understanding the heart orientation of teenagers. The passage shows the danger of making quick judgments. It is an encouragement to be aware of behavior that flows from the patterns and habits of the heart. This story reveals the need for careful observation of children's lives and attitudes so that parents can become a true refuge as their children grow and mature into adulthood. It is critical to discern the difference between actual rebellion and behavior that stems from a troubled heart.

IN SESSION COUNSELING

Read the parable of the two sons in Matthew 21:28–32 and ask parents the same question that Jesus asked regarding the responses of the two sons. "Which of the two did the will of his father?" The truly rebellious son is the one who deceptively manipulated his father by eagerly agreeing and then going on his own way. The first son revealed the struggle in his heart by expressing his resistance but afterward doing what he was asked to accomplish.

• How does this relate to your current situation?
• Have the parents missed a troubling event in his life?
• Has their direction to him been pleasant and respectful?
• Are their words structured to benefit or simply to command?
• How has your frustration in the situation hindered your relationship?
• What is the nature of their daily communication with him; do they listen to learn or to defend?

Challenge the parents to look beyond the initial negative responses of their son and seek to understand what is behind his resistance. Uses these thoughts as a springboard to help the parents begin to evaluate the true heart patterns of their son. Encourage them to identify areas for which they are grateful and areas in which they can lovingly communicate to their child in their struggle.

AFTER SESSION ASSIGNMENT

1. Prayerfully reflect on any difficult, unsettling, or unexpected changes that may have happened in the life of your son or your family.

2. Discuss ways you both can come together in helping your child with their heart struggles. How are you walking in unity?

3. Intentionally set aside time to talk and pray with your child about things that may be troubling them.

4. Ask your child if there is something in the way you are giving your direction that is difficult for them.

5. Make a concerted effort to show appreciation for the good things your child does and seek to speak to them in pleasant, gentle, respectful language. Review these scriptures together: Proverbs 15:1–2; 16:20–24, Phil. 2:3–4, Ephesians 4:29.

6. Keep a written log of these 4 steps and bring them to our next session for evaluation.

MATTHEW 26 36-46

& LUKE 22 40-46

JESUS TOUCHED BY TRAUMA

By: Brad Hambrick
www.bradhambrick.com

It may be easy for us to think that God Almighty in human flesh was so strong and so aware of his surroundings that Jesus could not be influenced by trauma. As we will see, that is not true. In his humanity, Jesus was heavily affected by the anticipation of the cross physically and emotionally. Jesus was sorrowful to the point of despairing of life (Matt. 26:38) and sweating drops of blood (Luke 22:44). We find in this passage a Savior who truly understands our challenges and an invitation to be honest about how trauma impacts us.

IN SESSION COUNSELING

Read Matthew 26:36–46 and Luke 22:40–46 aloud and discuss the following three questions.

What do we learn about trauma?

- *No amount of spiritual maturity prevents us from experiencing trauma.* Jesus was perfect and, at this moment, entering the climax of fulfilling God's purpose for his earthly life. Yet, even so, he experienced trauma and it struck him deeply.
- *Trauma is both an emotional and physical experience.* Jesus' body and mind were adversely affected by the traumatic weight of anticipating the cross.
- *Not everyone gets what we're going through.* The disciples didn't understand the significance or impact of what Jesus was going through. Even as the all-knowing God incarnate asked for their help during this experience, they didn't get it.

How did Jesus respond?

- Honest with the Father – Jesus didn't sugar coat how hard this was for him and that he wished there was another way. Even knowing there was no other way, Jesus asked anyway.
- Honest with Others – Jesus didn't hide his weakness from his friends. Jesus was not ashamed of his weakness; isolation would have only made his troubles greater. We see Jesus' strength in his willingness to be honest.
- Faithful – Jesus continued. In this case, Jesus' suffering was central to redemptive history, so he completed his mission. What it looks like for you to be faithful may be different. Honoring God's will in a situation can come by answering, "What does God want *from* me in this situation?" and "What does God want *for* me in this situation?" Allowing God to care for you in hard times is a form being faithful to God's agenda for that season of life.

What do we learn about faith in the hardest times?

- Holiness and weakness can coexist – The emotional and physical weakness of Jesus in Gethsemane no more marred his holiness than his lack of physical and emotional development as an infant in the Bethlehem manger. We too often mistake strength for character. God does not.
- Trauma is suffering, not sin – When we face trauma, God views us with compassion, not judgment. God offers comfort, not forgiveness, because trauma is not something to be repented of. It is easy to forget this when we've been through profoundly hard things.

• Honesty helps even when circumstances don't change – Jesus' honesty didn't prevent his friends from falling asleep or reroute his path from Calvary. But it kept him relationally connected, with God and friends, during a time when distrust and disillusionment were inevitably mounting.

AFTER SESSION ASSIGNMENT

1. *Be honest about weakness without shame.* What are the ways that your traumatic experience is adversely affecting you? Answer this question without feeling bad (i.e., guilty) because life is indeed hard.

2. *Be honest with God.* If you were going to pray as Jesus did in Matthew 26:39, what would you say? As you pray these things, visualize God attentively listening to you with eyes of compassion.

3. *Be honest with a friend.* If you were going to be honest with a friend as Jesus was in Matthew 26:38, what would you say? Who is the friend you trust enough to have this kind of conversation with?

4. *Seek wise care for your body and emotions.* Luke was a doctor; hence, he is the only one of the four gospel writers to record the detail about Jesus sweating drops of blood. Talk with a doctor to identify if there are ways to better care for your body and emotions as you recover from this trauma.

MARK 1
40-42

THE SAVIOR'S HEALING TOUCH

By: Beth Broom
www.bethmariebroom.com

MARK 1:40-42

In the first century, many diseases kept people from being able to function in daily life. Leprosy was a highly contagious disease in which the person often had to leave the community altogether and live outside the city. Some people with leprosy had almost no human interaction because of the threat of spreading the disease. The man in this passage boldly came toward Jesus with a request for healing, despite the cultural expectation that he remain secluded.

IN SESSION COUNSELING
Read Mark 1:40–42 and discuss the following questions.

What do we notice about the man with leprosy?
- He "implores" Jesus, demonstrating his earnestness and desperation.
- He kneels down, indicating that he humbly understands Jesus' power and authority to heal.
- We do not read that he was shy about doing this, even though it would have been culturally inappropriate for him to approach Jesus because of the spread of disease.

What do we notice about Jesus?
- He is moved with pity. This means he is compelled by the compassion he feels for this man's suffering.
- He touches the man. In other situations when Jesus heals, he demonstrates that he doesn't have to touch someone in order to heal. But He chooses to touch this man as part of the healing process.
- He speaks to the man, telling him that he is willing to cleanse him.

How does this relate?
- What stands out to you in this passage? What do you think and feel as you read it?
- Do you believe Jesus approaches your suffering in the same way He approached the man with leprosy? What makes you believe or not believe?
- How do you approach Jesus in your suffering? Is it similar to the way the man with leprosy approached Him? What compels you (or hinders you) in approaching Jesus?
- What would it be like for Jesus to touch the deepest place of suffering in your life?

AFTER SESSION ASSIGNMENT

1. Spend some time thinking and journaling about this passage. Here are some questions to consider:
   a. What needs the healing touch of Jesus in your life?
   b. Do you believe Jesus wants to heal you? Do you believe he can?
   c. What might hinder you from imploring Jesus and kneeling at his feet to ask for what you need?

2. Write a prayer to Jesus about your present suffering. You can say anything you want to say. He loves you and hears you, and his arms are open to you.

MARK4
35–41

REVEALING THE STRENGTH
OF OUR FAITH

By: Joy Forrest
www.calledtopeace.org

In Mark 4, Jesus' disciples response to a storm at sea revealed their lack of faith. Even though Jesus was right there with them, and though they had seen him perform many miracles, their response was sheer panic. This narrative shows us that the stress of negative circumstances can reveal what we truly believe. The storms reveal the strength of our faith.

IN SESSION COUNSELING

Read Mark 4:35–41 aloud and discuss the following questions.

What do we learn about the disciples in this narrative?
- They were following Jesus' leading.
- He was right there with them, but they were still overcome with fear.
- They questioned whether or not he cared about them and their circumstances.
- Their previous experiences with Jesus showed them that he could overcome the impossible, but they failed to believe he would do it for them.
- They were terrified after he calmed the storm. A fear of the Lord replaced their fear of impending harm.

What do we learn about Jesus?
- He had human limitations, and needed rest. He was so tired the storm did not wake him.
- He was human.
- He led the disciples to this place, and likely knew a storm was coming.
- He didn't panic about frightful circumstances, but took authority over them, showing his divine nature and sovereignty over the situation.
- He challenged the disciples for their lack of faith, and implied they could have chosen to believe.

What do you think was at the heart of the disciples' fear? See verse 38.
- They questioned whether or not he cared about them and their predicament. Adverse circumstances seem to have given them the impression that he wasn't concerned for their welfare. Perhaps they questioned his love altogether.
- Their question shows they may have even doubted his goodness, because he led them there and allowed the storm to happen.

AFTER SESSION ASSIGNMENT

1. Challenging circumstances can reveal what we truly believe about God. We may begin to question His care for us, and even question whether or not He is truly good—especially when we suffer after faithfully following Him. For many of us, a lack of faith is the result of not recognizing His good intentions toward us. Jesus' response to their panic suggested the disciples could have chosen to believe. When we are tempted to fear, rather than believe, we can choose to proclaim and act on truth from his Word (Psalm 56:3).

    a.   In what areas are you struggling that is revealing what you believe about God?

    b.   What has hindered you from trusting in the Lord and having faith in your circumstances?

2.   Read the following passages: Isaiah 41:10; 1 John 4:18; 1 Peter 5:7; Romans 8:15–16; and Hebrews 10:23. How do these verses connect knowing God's character to overcoming fear?

3.   Read Romans 8:28–39. What does this passage tell us about God's intentions toward us in suffering? How might understanding his sovereignty and goodness help us overcome fear? How can you choose to act on faith rather than fear?

4.   Take time to journal as you read the Scriptures and reflect on the questions. Bring this with you to the next session and review with your counselor.

NOTES

MARK 5

25-34

COURAGEOUS FAITH

By: Shauna Van Dyke
www.speakthetruth.org

During the time of this narrative, it was a law that men weren't allowed to speak to women in public because they were considered second-class citizens. Women were excluded from worship among men and were considered of less importance and value. In this Bible narrative, we see how Jesus showed value and love toward an unclean woman by giving her complete and instant healing because of her faith.

IN SESSION COUNSELING

Read Mark 5:25–34 aloud and discuss the following three questions.

What do we learn about the woman?

- She had been bleeding for 12 years. A bleeding issue at this time deemed her unclean (Leviticus 15), which meant she was unable to go anywhere and was unable to touch anything or anyone.
- She had suffered much under the care of many physicians and spent all she had but was only getting worse. She had no physical contact, no public worship, no financial means, was isolated, alone, and in a perpetual state of physical pain. Being an outcast for 12 years, excluded from everything and everyone, and with nothing left we can imagine she is discouraged and desperate for healing.

How does the woman respond?

- Courageously (v.27) – despite the crowd judging her as one not supposed to touch anyone, as an outcast and unclean, when she heard about Jesus she went to him.
- Faithfully (v.28) – she believed that even if she touched his garments she would be healed. Her faith produced a boldness to only see Jesus and not the limitations of her sickness to hold her back.
- Honestly (v. 33) – when confronted about what she had done, she fell before Jesus and answered truthfully.

What do we learn about Jesus?

- Jesus demonstrated his value for women - Remember how men were not to speak to women in public? When the woman touched his cloak, Jesus could have kept on walking and the healing would have been between just them. Instead, Jesus stopped and demonstrated his value for women by speaking to her.
- Jesus demonstrated his love for women - Remember how by being unclean she was to have no physical contact? When asked if she touched his cloak, her fear could have made her lie or run away. Instead, she fell before him and told the whole truth. His gentle response in calling her "daughter,' a term for believers and a team of endearment, demonstrated his love for women.
- Jesus commended her faith – Knowing already who touched his cloak, knowing he shouldn't have been touched, knowing it was against the law to speak to a woman in public, Jesus took the time to stop and lovingly speak to the courageous woman by acknowledging her faith and providing instant and complete healing.

AFTER SESSION ASSIGNMENT

1. Faith is putting our complete trust or confidence in something or someone. Genuine saving faith is in Jesus. What did you learn about faith from this passage?

2. Read Hebrews 11, Ephesians 2:8, and 1 Corinthians 2:5. What do you learn about faith from these passages? What other examples of faith did you see in Hebrews?

3. Is anything hindering you from going to Jesus and living in a courageous faith that trusts in Him and relies on Him fully and without reservation? What is a practical step you can take today?

LUKE 6

46–49

FAITHFUL OBEDIENCE

By: Emily Dempster
www.shccounseling.org

Amid struggles and suffering, counselees often do not see in what they are placing their hope, trust, confidence, and security. They strive to work harder, do better, and square up certain areas more, only to be disappointed and be lacking hope, joy, and peace. After spending time teaching the disciples about not just living according to the law but instead in faithful obedience toward God's purpose of the law, Jesus tells his disciples in Luke 6:46–49 to build their house upon a rock instead of sinking sand.

IN SESSION COUNSELING

Read Luke 6:46–49 aloud with your counselee.

Point 1: Jesus is contrasting those who just hear His words versus those who hear His words and obey them (verses 46–47).
- Compare the two ways of living – living life knowing about God or living life knowing God and being obedient to His Word.
- Ask: What would it look like in your life to obey the Word of God? What areas are difficult for you to obey?

Point 2: The man obedient to the Word of God is like a man who builds his house on a rock that is solid, and the foundation goes deep into the rock (verse 48a). The man who hears Jesus' words but does not obey is like a man who builds his house upon the ground without a foundation. Matthew 7:26 says he is like a man that builds his house upon the sand (verse 49a).
- Compare the two ways of building – building a house upon the foundation of God's Word and obedience to it, or building it on one's own thoughts, hopes, desires, and confidence.
- Ask: What foundation are you building your house on? The truths of God's Word or something else (a successful relationship, another person, financial security, health stability, etc.)?

Point 3: The storms of life are going to come (verses 48b and 49b). Jesus said, "In this world you will have trouble" (John 16:33). These storms might be small rainstorms, pelting floods, or hurricanes, but they will come. What matters in the storm is your foundation.
- Compare the two ways of facing the storm: walking in the storm on the rock or in the sand. What is the foundational difference?
- Ask: What storms are you facing right now? What does this reveal about your foundation?

Discuss what it might take to begin building a new foundation through obedience to God's Word.

AFTER SESSION ASSIGNMENT

1. Do an inventory of your life and the areas in which you put your hope, security, trust, confidence, and peace that are like sand (at any time could shift, change, or wash out). Make a list and include possible new areas you might have thought about since meeting with your counselor.

2. Reflect on the passage above about a solid foundation. Building a solid foundation requires hearing God's Word and obeying it. Journal about an area where you would like to grow in obedience or where you might be struggling.

3. Who in your life could offer you encouragement and accountability? Reach out to them for support and prayer.

LUKE17
11–19

THE GOD WHO HEALS

By: Susan Thomas
www.passionatelife.com

God is our ultimate Healer. God cares about our immediate needs, illnesses, and troubles, but God knows our greatest need is the healing of our souls. In this narrative, we see ten very sick men cry out to Jesus for physical healing. Jesus had mercy on them and healed their bodies as they stepped out in faith. Despite this huge blessing, only one man returned to give God glory. Only the man who placed his faith in Jesus as Lord received healing on earth and the complete, eternal healing of salvation.

IN SESSION COUNSELING
Read Luke 17:11–19 and discuss the following questions.

What do we learn about the ten men and how might their story apply to us?
- At this time, leprosy was a devastating diagnosis that attacked the body, leaving sores, missing fingers/toes, and damaged limbs. In addition to physical pain, these men faced horrific emotional pain at the loss of family, friends, and life as they knew it. NO ONE could be near them but other lepers slowly dying of the same disease.
- Describe your sick places. In what area(s) of your life are you experiencing deep pain right now? What loss have you experienced?

Lessons from the lepers.
- They believed Jesus could heal their bodies. They sought Jesus and cried out to Him.
- In verse14, we see them obey what Jesus told them to do. They obeyed Jesus *before* they could see their healing! They were healed ("cleansed") *as they went*.
- Sometimes God heals us in an instant. Sometimes God heals us *as we go* with Him.
- Having FAITH leads us to follow Jesus. Following Jesus *always leads to LIFE*.
- Only one man returned to Jesus to thank and praise God. While all 10 men had faith for physical healing, it appears that only one man had faith for eternal salvation.
- Sometimes we only focus on temporary needs/wants and neglect our ultimate need of Christ.

What do we learn about Jesus?
- Jesus had mercy on them and healed them. Jesus has the same heart of love for you today.
- Jesus answered their prayer and miraculously healed their bodies.
- Jesus had more healing available for these men, but only one experienced all Jesus offers. o Two different Greek words are used to describe healing. Vs 17: "Jesus asked, didn't I *heal* (katharizó: to cleanse) ten men?" Vs. 19: Jesus said to the man, "Stand up and go. Your faith has *healed* (sózó: to save) you." Physical healing is temporary. God wants to heal your soul *eternally*.

AFTER SESSION ASSIGNMENT

1. Re-read Luke 17:11–19 and ask the Holy Spirit to help you hear God's voice and apply His Word.

2. Do you identify with the nine men or the one man who returned to Jesus? Describe in detail.

3. Saving faith is your starting point. Have you placed your faith in Jesus as Lord and Savior?

4. Daily faith is key to living healthy and healed. Do you trust God as you go in your daily life?

5. Read verse 14. What specific things might God be asking you to do as you follow Him in faith this week?

6. Pray: "God help me not to only focus on or settle for temporary healing. Help me pursue Christ and your healing in every area and give glory to God for all of my life. In Jesus' name, Amen."

LUKE17
11–19

HOPE IN OUR SUFFERING

By: Rick Walton
www.truenorth.care

So that the reader can have the certainty described in Luke 1:4 and trust in Jesus and the apostolic teaching, Luke compiles a narrative from eyewitness accounts of Jesus. This Bible narrative is helpful in processing suffering because it gives us a certainty of hope across an extreme spectrum of suffering. A reason you would use this Scripture in a counseling session is for both you and your counselee to move through the context of suffering to the Savior.

Jesus chooses to travel from Galilee to Jerusalem (Lk. 9:51), which would culminate in his death and resurrection (Lk. 23:26–24:12). While this journey would normally take a couple of days, we locate Jesus en route on a southward trajectory walking for several months. He was somewhere between the two regions of Samaria and Galilee when he begins to enter an unknown village (17:11–12a).

IN SESSION COUNSELING

Read aloud Luke 17:11–19 on Jesus cleansing the ten lepers and discuss the following questions.

How could their life context influence the way they experienced living?
- The disease of leprosy anesthetizes the person from physically feeling, so that their nerves and nervous system do not communicate the warnings of pain. The community reasonably may have experienced the sorrow of loss combined with intense feelings of fear. In lieu of the disease's communicable nature, the leper was mandated to live in camps isolated from their family, jobs, and religious community. The trauma of living with a physical, painful sickness, coupled with the mental and emotional burden it imposes, must be a horrific form of suffering.
- Can you imagine the pain and suffering not only from being ostracized, but also from being constantly required to warn all passing by with the declaration, "unclean"? (Lev. 13:45–46; Num. 5:2).
- However, it is interesting to note that for some lepers, their immense suffering seemed to erase or minimize ethnic prejudices. How might their suffering influence a willingness to love and care for one another, more than to express sinful ethnic prejudice?

What do Jesus' actions teach about his response to cries for help in suffering?
- Jesus sees them in their situation. He hears their cries for mercy. Elsewhere, Jesus moved towards the leper and touched him (Lk. 5:12–16).
- Jesus spoke directly to them, and cleansed these lepers on his own terms. In the gospels, Jesus applies various methods alongside his supernatural ability to heal physical infirmity (Lk. 4:31–41; 5:12–26; 6:6–11; 7:1–17; 8:26–56; 9:37–43; 13:10–17).
- How do Jesus' actions evoke a response from the lepers to trust him for physical healing?

What do the ten lepers' actions teach about their desire for hope in suffering?

*   The ten lepers were united in seeking relief from their suffering. However, only one leper wanted more than mere physical relief, and desired relationship with Jesus for eternal hope (Lk. 17:15–19; Jn. 11:25).
*   The miracles of Jesus pointed beyond mere physical deliverance to salvation of the whole person (Mt. 10:28). Faith in Jesus was more than a miracle worker; it meant being the Son of God and Savior unto eternal life (Lk. 9:18–20; Jn. 3:16; 20:30–31).
*   What does this Luke 17: 11–19 teach about discerning one's motives in seeking Jesus in suffering?

AFTER SESSION ASSIGNMENT

Journal daily for two weeks (cycle through the questions twice), and discuss your answers in your next counseling session.

*   Day 1: Where have my thoughts been lingering in my suffering?

*   Day 2: What emotions am I most commonly feeling deeply in my suffering?

*   Day 3: What physical symptoms or experiences do I believe are connected to my suffering?

*   Day 4: How have my relationships with family, church, and coworkers been impacted or changed in my suffering?

*   Day 5: Where is God in my situation? How would I describe my thoughts and feelings about God in my suffering?

*   Day 6: What have I been crying out to Jesus for in my suffering? What really are my motives in seeking after God?

*   Day 7: What are two things, over the past week, that I am grateful to God for?

NOTES

LUKE 19
1–10

THE FRUIT OF REPENTANCE

By: Carl Chica
www.R3stored.com

In the book of Luke, we encounter the narrative of Zacchaeus and his transformative interaction with Jesus. By understanding some of his background it helps us to better understand the incredible heart transformation that he experiences. Zacchaeus was a tax collector in the region of Jericho and was described as a financially affluent man. As a Jewish man in his position in the service of Rome he would be a man considered a sinner and betrayer of his own people. Jewish tax collectors were known as cheaters and traitors.

IN SESSION COUNSELING

Read Luke 19:1–10 together and work through the questions below. Be patient with the counselee and allow them time to think through each area of interaction compared to their own heart.

Zacchaeus wanted to see Jesus as He passed through town, but, because Zacchaeus was a short man, he could not see over the crowd. Knowing that Jesus would pass by a certain sycamore tree, Zacchaeus ran ahead and climbed up the tree, hoping he could see Jesus. His desire to see Jesus is very interesting. First, Zacchaeus did not think himself important enough for Jesus to notice him. Second, he understood his position and what he represented within his community. Zacchaeus was totally caught off guard when Jesus stopped under the tree, looked up, and said, "Zacchaeus, hurry and come down, for I must stay at your house today." This may have been the first time anyone, much less the Messiah, had ever shown him grace and mercy.

- *What are you known as? Your reputation with others and more importantly Jesus.*
- *In what ways does Jesus impact your life?*

Interacting with Jesus transforms who we are. The more time we spend with Him the more we look less like ourselves and more like him. There are four areas to highlight that show how this interaction with Jesus will transform Zacchaeus from a sinner to a friend of Jesus.

Recognizes: Zacchaeus recognizes who Jesus really is. And he recognizes his unworthiness of the grace and mercy extended to him. He is a sinner and in need of forgiveness.
- *In what areas are you in need of forgiveness?*
- *Do you feel unworthy to be a friend of Jesus?*

Reasons: Zacchaeus doesn't deserve grace and Jesus is the only one that can make things right. He must believe in the one who offers this grace and mercy.
- *How did Jesus show Zacchaeus grace in this passage?*
- *How do you think Jesus has shown you grace?*

Repents: To repent requires a change of direction/heart. Zacchaeus understands his need to live differently from his past.
- *Is there anything you would like to repent of?*
- *Whether it's from your past or a current sin, we can go to the Lord together right now.*

Replaces: Zacchaeus' heart transformation and repentance produce the "fruit of repentance" in the form of thoughts, desires, and actions that seek to make things right with those he has sinned against and to perform these in a lavish way. Since Jesus loves and offers forgiveness to sinners in a lavish way he must also follow in the Messiah's footsteps. Past ways of thinking, desiring, and behaving are replaced with the Fruit of the Spirit. (Galatians 5:22–23)

- *In what ways does your thinking, desires and choices need to be transformed?*
- *Let's pray for the fruit of the Spirit in your life.*

AFTER SESSION ASSIGNMENT

This week read Luke 19:1–10 again and continue praying through the questions we discussed in session. Ask the Lord to reveal new areas for change.

What areas of your life does Jesus want to transform? What attitudes, strong desires, and patterns of sin?

- **Recognize:** Name an area you recognize Jesus wants you to grow and change.

- **Reason:** Consider where your thoughts and/or actions are inconsistent with the grace and mercy you have received.

- **Repent:** In what ways do you need to change direction? Change thinking and submit desires? Change behaviors?

- **Replace:** In what ways do you need to replace Jesus as the rightful king and ruler of your life?

JOHN 4
1-30

JESUS AND THE WOMAN OF SAMARIA

By: Jesse Pirkle
www.sohillscc.com

Jesus has left Judea and is on His way to Galilee. He decides to travel through Samaria and enters Sychar, where He meets a Samaritan woman drawing water. Jews and Samaritans did not typically associate with one another, which makes this encounter especially intriguing. Jesus' interaction with her reveals His care for every kind of person. What can we learn from this passage?

IN SESSION COUNSELING
Read John 4:1-30 aloud and discuss the following questions.

What do we learn about the woman?
- She is at the well at noontime. This is certainly not the ideal time to make this journey. Almost certainly, she is trying to avoid interacting with other people (perhaps from fear and/or shame).
- She is surprised that Jesus, a Jewish man, would stop and speak with her.
- She has had five husbands, and she is currently with a man who is not her husband. For whatever reason, this likely has to do with her being at the well at noon. The situation with the six men, in some sense, has formed much of her lifelong identity (in verse 29, she says that Jesus "told me *all* that I *ever* did" (italics added).

What do we learn about Jesus?
- He is tired and thirsty. Jesus is truly human.
- Jesus arrives at this well precisely with intent to speak with this woman. This interaction is sovereignly orchestrated. Jesus knows this woman with intimate detail. He is truly God.
- Jesus offers her a kind of water that eternally satisfies.
- Jesus does not sweep her current sin under the rug. He brings it up to her, instructs her on proper worship (in spirit and in truth), and reveals Himself to her as the Messiah.

What implications does this have for us?
- First, comfort. This seemingly random, sinning Samaritan woman who wanted to hide was sought out by Jesus. He sought her out and offered her a new kind of water. Our Lord cares about us individually, regardless of how we are treated by our culture.
- True worship comes from the heart, not a specific mountain or church building. We are safe to assume her life and identity significantly changed based on her interaction with Jesus. She leaves her water jar (v. 28), and many Samaritans believed in Jesus because of her testimony (v. 39). She is no longer hiding, but actively sharing about the Messiah.

AFTER SESSION ASSIGNMENT

1. What in your life has shaped your identity? If Jesus were to "tell you all you've ever done" what would that include?

2. How has your old identity been unsatisfying? What well do you need to stop returning to?

3. Read Psalm 34. Pray that verse 8 would be true for you, and that the Lord Himself would satisfy you in ways that the world never can.

JOHN 4
1-30

TRANSFORMING REPENTANCE

By: Margaret Ashmore
www.margaretashmore.com

"Repentance is a pure gospel grace. The covenant of works admitted no repentance; there it was, sin and die. Repentance came in by the gospel. Christ has purchased in His blood that repenting sinners shall be saved. Thus, repentance is a doctrine that has been brought to light only by the gospel.[1]" Indeed, repentance is that moment on which God awaits that He may bestow real and radical transformation in the believer's life. But what does biblical repentance look like?

IN SESSION COUNSELING

Read John 4:1–30 thoughtfully, and with careful meditation consider the following.

When did the woman at the well encounter Jesus?

- It was the "sixth hour" which would have been noon. She had lived her whole life in the shadows of sin and shame but the Light of the World will expose her sin, not for condemnation but for redemption.
- She had come to the well at a place called "Sychar" whose meaning in Greek is "end." That's where she found herself, at the end of all her efforts to ever find peace, or joy or freedom from her past. She was at the end of "self."
- She had come thirsty, parched from the wasteland of sin that had promised her satisfaction but had always left her, like her waterpot, empty. She was ready for a Savior.

How did Jesus draw this frightened, suspicious, defeated woman to himself?

- He never once pointed out her sin. He knew how fragile was her heart. The conversation began naturally, not theologically. He even interrupted her when she began to talk about her past to spare her of the sordid details. Furthermore, He sent His disciples into the city to protect her from any further looks of contempt or disapproval. Oh, what a shelter is our Savior!
- The Word made flesh was showing her that the Bible doesn't even recognize determinism, that we have to be what our past dictates, but only transformation.

What is your Sychar? What is your waterpot?

- So, where do you need to come to at the end of all your strategies to find real change and deep satisfaction in your life apart from God? Have you ceased from manipulation? Self-pity? Anger when people disappoint you? Isolation when you have unconfessed sin in your life? It is only at Sychar that you will find the transforming grace of Jesus.
- After the woman at the well met Jesus and received the Living Water of the soul reviving Gospel, the Bible says, "She left her waterpot behind." This is the most beautiful and clear picture of repentance in Scripture.
- What is your waterpot? What do you need to leave behind? A sinful relationship? Harboring bitterness? Looking at pornography? Resentments of the past? Because you now have the Living Water, because you now have the Bread of Life, because you now have the pure Gospel grace of Christ's forgiveness, repent and leave it behind as you shout to the world about the unconditional love of God, "*Come see a Man Who knows all about me*" and still loves me!

---

[1]Quote by Thomas Watson, from The Doctrine of Repentance, 1668; Banner of Truth

AFTER SESSION ASSIGNMENT

1. Prayerfully go the Lord and ask him to reveal the ways you are still trying to change yourself apart from true repentance. Ask him to show you the waterpots you are still clinging to and for the grace to leave them behind.

2. On the other side of repentance, of leaving behind "self" is a life filled with Christ!

NOTES

JOHN
7 53– 8 11

THE SAVIOR'S HEALING TOUCH

By: Beth Broom
www.bethmariebroom.com

During Jesus' days of ministry, the scribes and Pharisees (Jewish leaders and teachers) made a habit of asking questions of Jesus in order to catch Him in a lie or make Him look foolish. Their goal was to discredit Him in front of the Jewish people. Imagine yourself in the scene of this passage. Jesus is teaching at the temple early in the morning. People are gathered all around, and suddenly the scribes and Pharisees show up dragging a woman with them. She is disheveled and frightened. They interrupt Jesus' teaching to ask him what they should do with her, since the Law states she should be stoned to death for committing adultery. All eyes are on Jesus to see how he will respond.

IN SESSION COUNSELING
Read John 7:53–8:11 and discuss the following questions:

What stands out?
- As you read the passage, what do you notice about the woman? about Jesus? about the scribes and Pharisees?
- What do you think the woman expects to happen? What do the scribe and Pharisees expect?
- What is surprising about how Jesus responds?

How does this relate?
- Picture yourself in this scene.
  - What would you have thought and felt if you had been the woman caught in adultery?
  - What would you have thought and felt if you had been a part of the crowd?
  - What would you have thought and felt if you had been one of the scribes/Pharisees?
- What does this passage tell you about Jesus' character?
- What is the primary message Jesus wants the woman to hear and learn? Is this a message you believe, or is it difficult for you to believe?

As the counselor, be prepared to prompt the counselee to think about Jesus' nearness, comfort, and love. The go-to thought for a lot of counselees is that Jesus is angry or disappointed in them when they sin. While Jesus hates our sin, He doesn't shun or reject us. This passage is a beautiful picture of how Jesus doesn't ignore the sin but still shows compassion and love for the woman.

AFTER SESSION ASSIGNMENT

1. Spend some time thinking and journaling about this passage. Here are some questions to consider:
   a. The woman experienced Jesus' compassion and forgiveness. How have you experienced these things in your life?

b. In what ways do you struggle to believe that Jesus has compassion for you and forgives you?

2. We can imagine that this woman experienced something very intimate and deep when she encountered Jesus. Sometimes we struggle to encounter him in this way. Write a prayer to him, expressing your desire (and perhaps difficulty) to experience his presence and comfort. Ask him for what you need, and express your gratitude that he never leaves you or forsakes you.

JOHN10

22-30

THE JESUS I WANT OR THE JESUS I NEED

By: Laura Chica
www.Re3stored.org

IN SESSION COUNSELING

Read John 10:22–30, provide the overview points of the text to your counselee, and review the questions together. This might need to be broken into two separate sessions.

Point 1: Many Israelites believed that when Messiah came he would trample their oppressors, the Romans, and fulfill their desire to self-govern and rule Israel. All felt the fear and burden of Roman rule and the alleviation of this fear would be welcomed and celebrated. If there was a perfect time to start a revolt against the Romans, the Feast of Dedication—a memorial celebration of the successful Maccabean revolt—was it.

Some of those listening to Jesus were unable to contain their growing excitement. They gathered around Him and demanded, "How long will you keep us in suspense? If you are the Christ, tell us plainly."

Their anticipation was palpable: Are you Messiah? Are you the One who will free us from our pain and suffering, our bondage and oppression? Will you alleviate our problems and fulfill our dreams? Their enquiry ("*if* you are…") indicates that they see Jesus as a potential messiah, but they want Him on their own terms to fulfill their own purposes.

Their desires and fears were like our own—focused on current circumstances. We all want alleviation of our pain, sorrow, difficulty, and fear, while also experiencing the fulfillment of all our desires. We all want a messiah we can control.

- What desires and fears do you currently wrestle with?
- In what ways do you hope that Jesus will help alleviate or fulfill those desires and fears?

Point 2: "Jesus, knowing their hearts, answered them and said, 'I told you, and you do not believe. The works that I do in my Father's name bear witness about me, but you do not believe because you are not among my sheep'" (John 10:25-26, ESV).

Notice Jesus states that he *had* spoken clearly, he *had* made His mission plain, clear, and understandable. He is Messiah, the Anointed One, the son of God. The incredible miracles he performed bore witness to who he is. But those who were asking did not believe him—not because he had not made himself known; they could see that He was powerful and could perform great miracles, signs, and wonders.

They did not believe because he was not the messiah they were looking for. They wanted a messiah that matched their own heart's desire to conquer and rule. They wanted a messiah who looked, thought, and acted like themselves—a reflection of fallen man, created in their own likeness—someone who would fulfill their desires and minimize their fears.

- In what ways do you appreciate Jesus as He has made Himself known through His Word?
- In what ways do you struggle with what the Bible says about who Jesus is?
- In what ways do you expect Jesus to solve your problems and alleviate your suffering, grant your desires, and fulfill your dreams?

Point 3: Jesus continued, "My sheep hear my voice, and I know them, and they follow me." The evidence of faith is hearing the voice of the Shepherd and following Him. Jesus says that they could not hear because they did not have spiritual ears to hear. They could physically hear his words but they could not spiritually discern what they meant. They could not hear his voice because they were not "his" sheep. They did not believe in him.

- Do you hear the voice of the Shepherd? Do you hear and follow Jesus?
- Or, do you hear the voice of the Shepherd but follow what seems right to you—your own thinking, the philosophies of the world, the ideologies of our culture?

Point 4: Scripture is clear that those who hear his voice also follow him, or obey his commandments, his laws, his ways.

- In what ways do you claim to hear but fail to obey?
- How do you assess if you are his sheep and that he knows you?

Point 5: Jesus changes the focus of the conversation from the kingdom of this world—the current circumstances and relationships we experience here on Earth—to His eternal Kingdom. Despite what we wish and sometimes believe, Jesus did not come to alleviate our suffering. These are the products of a greater enemy than Rome. Jesus knows our greater enemy, the one that we often don't recognize: sin.

Sin wields its evil influence bringing with it pain, destruction, oppression, and death. Our sin would separate us from God for eternity. Jesus knew this and that is why He died on the cross and, in great victory, conquered sin forever!

- In what ways do you recognize the real enemy (sin) and the effects of its oppression and bondage in your current circumstances and relationships?
- How does knowing Jesus impact this enemy (sin) in your life?

Point 6: Jesus was the Messiah but he had not come to do what the Jewish leaders or the crowds wanted. He came to defeat Satan, sin, and death, and in so doing he offers us what we all want, *life*.

- Where do you seek life? From the world, circumstances and relationships?
- In what ways do you seek Jesus as the ultimate fulfillment, life in him?

Jesus concludes his response in John 10:28–30, saying, "I give them [my sheep who hear my voice and follow me] eternal life, and they will never perish, and no one will snatch them out of my hand. My Father, who has given them to me, is greater than all, and no one is able to snatch them out of the Father's hand. I and the Father are one" (ESV). Jesus promises eternal life, and security in Him.

- How does Jesus' promise of eternal life and the incredible security of being in both his and the Father's care impact your perspective on your current circumstances?

Point 7: This is our great hope! The Shepherd offers us ultimate fulfillment and freedom, not from the suffering and brokenness, or oppression of this world, but freedom from the desires and fears of our hearts. He offers us Himself. "I sought the LORD, and He answered me; He delivered me from all my [internal] fears. Those who look to Him are radiant with joy; their faces shall never be ashamed" (Psalm 34:4–5, BSB).

Alleviation of the difficulties we face is not necessary to our peace when we follow the One who promises that our soul will never perish and that no one can remove us from his hand or from the Father's hand. Each of us, held securely in the precious nail-pierced hands of our Shepherd who gave His life for His sheep, "shall not want" (Psalm 23:1) for true *life* again.

- The ultimate question is, do I want my own version of Jesus, who I hope will alleviate my suffering and fulfill my desires? Or do I want the real Jesus, who calls me to follow Him in obedience even through the pain and the suffering?
- Am I seeking the Jesus I need, or the Jesus I want?

AFTER SESSION ASSIGNMENT

Read John 10:22–30 again and continue to reflect on the in-session questions. Pray and journal what the Lord continues to reveal in your heart. Bring to your next session to review with your counselor.

NOTES

JOHN 11
1-44

HOPE IN OUR SUFFERING

By: Alicia McCamy
www.sohillscc.com

John 11 shows us a picture not only of Jesus' divine power, but of his heart and compassion for those who are hurting. Jesus draws near to us in our pain and sympathizes with our suffering. We can take hope that he has a purpose for our suffering, although certainly in doing so Jesus does not minimize our pain in the moment. Jesus is deeply moved by the suffering we experience and he grieves with us. This narrative is important in helping us learn to grieve with God by our side and to understand Jesus' nearness to us in the pain.

IN SESSION COUNSELING

Summarize John 11:1–27. Jesus receives word that his friend Lazarus is sick. Jesus did not go to Lazarus right away and predicted in verse 4 that this encounter would demonstrate the glory of God more than the restoration of sickness. When Jesus arrives Lazarus has been dead for four days. Martha, one of Lazarus' sisters, approaches Jesus about how if he had been there her brother would not have died. They have a beautiful interaction where Martha expresses her faith in Jesus' power to raise the dead.

Read John 11:28–44 and then review the following sections and questions.

Verses 28–32: Martha goes to get her sister Mary to bring her to Jesus. What do you notice about Mary's interaction with Jesus? Have you had similar questions to God about your pain? What has crying out to God looked like for you? What have you expressed to God about your specific suffering?

Verses 33–36: Jesus sees the pain of those who loved Lazarus and are now hurting. What is Jesus' response? What conclusions can we make about Jesus' care for those who are in pain in this story? What truths can we then conclude about how Jesus cares for us in our suffering?

Verses 37–44: Jesus continues to be moved by this scene and the grief of those around him. Finally, Jesus goes to the tomb and in a show of God's glory for the people, Jesus raises Lazarus from the dead. Jesus had healed the sick up until this point, but he had never publicly raised someone from the dead. What impact do you think this had on those who were there? What does it say about Jesus' power?

Conclusion:
In this text we see that Jesus loved them (11:5), he was deeply moved and greatly troubled (11:33) over their pain. There was something greater than their grief that Jesus had in mind for them to see and understand. Through their belief they saw the glory of God in Lazarus's restoration to life. We can be confident that while God has a purpose for our pain, he does not overlook our hurt. It is unlikely that God has plans to raise our friends and family from the dead, but God does have a purpose for all the trials we face. He cares for us. Believing and trusting in him, we find peace and joy in the delays.

AFTER SESSION ASSIGNMENT

1. Reflect that Jesus weeps with you in your pain. Take a few moments this week to stop and consider this truth. Sit in a quiet space and reflect on this in silence for ten minutes. Set a timer if you need to help focus your time.

2. Bring your pain to Jesus this week. Journal the questions you have for God about your situation and conclude your journal by asking God to comfort you in your pain and to help you see His power for your pain.

3. Consider how Jesus is using your pain. Write out 10-12 ways that God could be using your situation to teach you something or to use your story for His glory. Pray to the Lord for help and comfort as you seek to glorify Him.

JOHN13
1–5

INSTRUCTION & COMFORT FROM OUR BETRAYED SAVIOR

By: Eliza Huie
www.elizahuie.com

JOHN 13:1–5

John 13:1–5 Jesus washes the disciples' feet.

In this narrative we see an extraordinary example of humility and trust. Knowing the cross is before him, Jesus prepares to have supper with his disciples. Judas is one of them. What happens in this passage not only instructs us but also comforts us. Through his example, Jesus instructs us on how we can respond to the bitter sting of betrayal. Through his experience, Jesus comforts us with the reality that he understands how difficult it is to love our enemies. This brief biblical narrative holds profound truth that can help and encourage your counselee.

IN SESSION COUNSELING
Read John 13:1–5 and discuss the following points.

How does this passage instruct us from the example of Jesus?
- Humble sacrifice is what we are called to. Jesus demonstrated a humility toward his disciples that was not dependent on their actions. (vs. 1)
- The Father is trustworthy. In the midst of the most difficult situations, Jesus trusts the Father. (vs. 3)
- Humility is always an appropriate response. At a time when Jesus most deserved to be served, he served others. (vv. 4–5)

How does this passage comfort us from the example of Jesus?
- Jesus exemplifies the path of humility that we are called to.
- Jesus knows the pain of betrayal.
- Jesus trusts the Father.
- Jesus was moved to act humbly not because of his circumstances but in spite of his circumstances.

Questions to ask in your session from this passage.
- How does Jesus knowing what is in the heart of Judas impact you as you consider your own betrayal? How does this instruct you in your own interaction with those who have betrayed you?
- When you face difficult situations is it a comfort to know that the Father has a plan? Do you trust His plan? How do your actions display trust or lack of trust in the Father?
- What might humility look like in your own situation of betrayal? What do you think moved Jesus to act with such humility in this situation? How might what motivated Him, motivate your actions as well?

Caution: This passage can be helpful when counseling someone facing betrayal in a non-abusive relationship. If the person is in an abusive relationship the questions and prompts should be used. For direction on this see the book *Is It Abuse?* by Darby Strickland.

AFTER SESSION ASSIGNMENT

Journal through these questions and discuss at your next counseling session.

1. How does this act of humble service remind you of what Jesus was willing to do to save you?

2. What did you learn from reading this story of Jesus washing the feet of his disciples?

3. How does knowing that Jesus faced betrayal bring encouragement to your situation?

4. How does Jesus' handling of betrayal instruct you in your own situation?

5. What act of humility might the Lord be encouraging you to take this week?

NOTES

JOHN 15
1–11

ABIDING FROM IDENTITY

By: Lee Lewis
www.soulcareconsulting.com

This story is one of the more famous metaphors that Jesus uses. It starts with the last of the seven "I am" statements that Jesus declares about himself in the Gospels. It is the only "I am" statement that draws in God the Father. Jesus is teaching and building off John 14. His final hours before his death are approaching and he is making clear that all he declares and does is in obedience to the Father. This is the key to understanding the call to abide.

IN SESSION COUNSELING
Read John 15:1–11 aloud and discuss the following three questions.

What is the significance of Jesus calling himself the "true vine"?
- Vine/vineyard language is used in multiple places in the Old Testament to describe Israel (God's chosen people). This statement by Jesus is a direct connection to Isaiah 5:1 that talks about a vineyard that God planted. This vineyard was planted in the most fertile of places and was protected, but it produced sour grapes. They could not yield good fruit.
- Jesus uproots Israel as the focus of God's redemptive plan. Jesus is saying *I am the only way to truth, life, salvation and redemption.*

What role does the vinedresser play in the metaphor?
- The vinedresser is the master gardener who cleans, spades, clears, plants, prunes, and fertilizes the garden. It is the picture of holistic cultivation and care. The Father is in ultimate control in overseeing the pruning work of the branches that Jesus has brought life to.
- It is the picture of the theological concepts of vivification and mortification. Vivification is to bring life and health to the soul, whereas mortification is to remove or put to death those things that rob the soul of life. The vinedresser brings into our lives that which will bring more fruit and he prunes and removes those things that take life from us.

What does it mean to abide? How does the call to abide fit with the role of the vine and vinedresser?
- Abiding means to receive, believe, trust, rest, and enjoy the Word of Christ. It is to stay in and under the Gospel of Christ.
- Jesus (the true vine) is the only true source of Life. God the Father (the vinedresser) is in complete control of the cultivating work that brings fruit from our life in Christ. Abiding is to look to and submit to Christ alone as Savior and to stay under his Word. Abiding is to stay under the cultivating work of the Father who always brings life and fruit from his cultivating work in our lives.
- Part of abiding is to enjoy all the benefits of salvation. Jesus says in verse 3 "already you are clean." This statement has identity implications. Christ cleans us, the Father prunes us, and we do nothing to be in the vine. We are grafted in (Rom. 11:17). We don't abide to get or earn anything from Jesus. We abide (enjoy, believe, receive) because we have life in him and are clean.

AFTER SESSION ASSIGNMENT

1. Abiding in Christ is to place our heart, faith, and allegiance under his Lordship. It also means we remain under the blade of pruning knowing that God prunes to bring more life and fruit. What did you learn about abiding that has implications for your life?

2. Something to consider about abiding is that it is a heart posture. This means that if we are not abiding in Christ then our abiding (trust, allegiance, rest, joy) is something other than God. When you are not abiding in Christ, where do you place your allegiance?

3. God the Father is the all-knowing vinedresser who never harms his children. Any pruning he brings into our lives is for more fruit. It is for our good. Where do you resist his pruning work in your life? Ask the Lord to help you trust his pruning work in your life. Lean in. Don't resist his cultivating care.

ACTS 15
36–41

WHEN MINISTRY PARTNERS PART WAYS

By: Chara Donahue
www.charadonahue.com

Even though we strive for peace with friends and partners in ministry, sometimes even Christians have sharp disagreements. That is where Barnabas and Paul find themselves in Acts 15 where they met shortly after Paul's conversion. Barnabas, who is called the son of encouragement in Acts 4, defends Paul to those who only knew his ruthless reputation (Acts 9:26-28). In Acts 11 and 13 we see Barnabas help Paul/Saul grow and watch Paul lead Barnabas as they travel together as missionaries carrying the hope of the Gospel. But their partnership comes to an abrupt conclusion over how they see ministry proceeding.

IN SESSION COUNSELING
Read Acts 15:36–41 together and discuss the following points.

What does Barnabas want to do?
*   Verse 37 tells us, "Now Barnabas wanted to take with them John called Mark." *A little about John Mark*: John Mark is Barnabas' cousin and likely the man who later served as Peter's secretary for writing what we call the Gospel of Mark. He may also be the naked guy fleeing the garden when Jesus is arrested (Mark 14:51–52).

Why is Paul concerned about taking John Mark along?
*   Verse 38 says, "But Paul thought best not to take with them one who had withdrawn from them in Pamphylia and had not gone with them to the work." Paul is concerned that because Mark deserted them out of fear before, he may desert them again, hindering their mission.

Are the scriptures clear about who is right in this instance?
*   No. People often assume that Paul is correct because Luke follows Paul's journey. This is an error in logic. Luke gives no indication about who chose rightly here. He simply says that Barnabas took Mark and Paul took Silas.

Barnabas' right belief in second chances and assurance that God can change people clashes with Paul's good desire to go boldly and efficiently with the Gospel. Our most deeply held convictions often reflect *what* and *how* we worship. They can be core values integral to who God created us to be. These aspects of our character help us to be faithful image-bearers of God, and sometimes these matters of conscience make it difficult to see how to respond. God desires unity between his people, but there are times when partnerships must come to an end because the mission God has for each individual differs from the path they planned together. It seems that in this circumstance, for both Barnabas and Paul to yield would be failing to do the right thing. James 4:17 teaches that if a believer fails to do what is right it is called sin. And Paul writes in Romans 14 that believers may honor God differently in how they live and respond to situations. The tricky part is discerning the difference between what is right—how each individual is called to honor God—and what is sin.

Counselor Consideration: In the situation the counselee is facing, is it clear who is right?

- If *it is unclear*, continue discussing the prior paragraph, even if it's something to discuss in a next session. Help counselees to discern: Is the conflict caused by fleshly desires or conflicting convictions? Is it possible to submit to the other out of love (see Ephesians 5:21 and Philippians 2:3-4)? Once the situation has become clearer you can move to the next step below.
- If *it is clear*, refer to the homework section for Scriptures on what to do when we sin against others or are sinned against. Ask counselees, "Ideally, how would you like to see this situation resolve?" Let's see what happens after Paul and Barnabas separate.

Ministry doesn't stop for either Paul or Barnabas. Instead, it multiplies. They both take a new companion and reach more people. In 1 Corinthians 9:6 Paul speaks of Barnabas' continued ministry. Luke continues to document Paul's ministry and the epistles show us even more. Read 2 Timothy 4:11. What does this show us about what happens to Mark?

We must always remember that God is at work in ways we do not fully comprehend. The loss of a friend due to a sharp disagreement is worth grieving, but we must also keep our eyes open for what God will do. God may open new doors, He may take people away so He can bring them back prepared, and He will always glorify His name if we trust Him with each step.

How do you think God is asking you to trust Him within this circumstance?

Make sure to end the session with prayer that God would strengthen your counselee to trust Him with what they say.

AFTER SESSION ASSIGNMENT

1. Conflict between humans is bound to happen in a fallen world. While there are situations where the disagreement stems from convictions, most people will be sinned against and sin against others. There are passages of Scripture that instruct believers on how to handle conflict when sinned against (Matthew 18:15–20) and when we sin against another (Matthew 5:23–24). Take some time to read these two passages and respond to the following questions:
   a. When you sin against another person, what would God have you do to seek reconciliation?
   b. When you have been sinned against, how does the Lord want you to respond?

2. Read Romans 12:18 and Ephesians 4:1–3. In your current situation, have you done everything you can to live in peace with this person and, in humility, seek unity with them? Pray that the Lord reveals an area of bitterness or resentment. Discuss this with your counselee in the next session.

ACTS 17

16-34

REPENTANCE FOR MISPLACED WORSHIP

By: Dr. Todd Hardin

www.thinkingchristianly.com

Since the beginning, human beings have been worshipers. However, since Genesis 3, we have all struggled with misplaced worship. The Bible calls misplaced worship idolatry, and this idolatry is insidious in that it often hides itself from the worshiper. All idolaters think they are pleasing God. However, idolatry lies at the heart of most problems people bring to counseling. How is it that so many Christians are having such a tough time in life? The problem flows from their worship where they have misunderstood themselves, their problem, and the solution to their problem. A careful examination of Paul's visit to Athens in Acts 17:16–34 can clear up these misunderstandings. In this passage, we learn that we seek (vv. 16–27a), we stumble (vv. 27b–29), but God saves (vv. 30–34). As counselees understand their inherent religiosity, inevitable tendency toward sin, and God's redemptive application of the Gospel, they will be better equipped to reorient their worship to God.

IN SESSION COUNSELING

Begin by saying something such as, *"You know, we often struggle with things we really care about. I can tell that you really value _____. Let's look at a passage of Scripture together that should help us clarify your position in relation to your problem."* After reading the passage Acts 17:16–34, explain:

"It seems to me that we are all innately religious. It appears that we will find something in which to place our affections. Now, we don't have a monument to an unknown god as the Athenians did, but we do tend to spend a great deal of time, attention, and money on things other than God. And the funny thing is, we often can't see that our devotion to these things is a little out of balance."

Counselor Consideration: As you are explaining how we are all like the Athenians in that we often find ourselves misplacing our worship, check to see if the counselee tracks with you. Then, ask how the Athenians' struggle with idolatry is similar to the problem he or she is experiencing.

"We find ourselves tying our happiness to these things and we feel betrayed if we are not rewarded for our faithfulness. We somehow feel cheated if the object of our affection doesn't deliver what we demand."
• What do you think is the current object of your affection?

"Now, that's the bad news. But, the good news is, once we are aware that we are loving something other than God too much, we can return to Him by turning and trusting Him as the ultimate object of our affections. The Bible calls this turning and trusting repentance and faith, and it is God's solution to misplaced worship."
• Would you like to pray together right now for the Lord's guidance and strength to help you turn your affections back to Him and to trust Him in your struggle?

Counselor Consideration: As you probe into this area of the counselee's life, anticipate defensiveness. None of us likes to be accused of idolatry. Do not let this dissuade you. Maintain a spirit of gentleness (see 2 Tim 2:24–26), but lovingly place the burden of proof on the counselee to explain how his or her problem is not a problem of worship.

AFTER SESSION ASSIGNMENT

1. Make a list of ways counselees' religiosity expresses itself in everyday life. For example, have them take a look at their calendars and bank transactions so they can see where they are spending their time and money. These places are good starting points for uncovering hidden idols. They may also shed light on the problem that brought the person to counseling.

2. After shedding light on the idols, in the previous step, have counselees list the ways the idol has let them down in making their lives better. Usually, idols promise freedom but deliver slavery. Have counselees identify how the idol has enslaved them.

3.   Ask counselees to bring the two lists to the next session. In that session, help them identify areas of repentance and help them work through the repentance process. Then, help them devise new habits of worship that will help them refocus on God.

ROMANS 6 12–14

& 2 TIMOTHY 2 22

RUN TOWARD RIGHTEOUSNESS

By: Andrew Dealy
www.AustinStoneCounseling.org

Sin was never meant to be our main focus. We were made for God. We were made to see and enjoy Him as we live life according to His beautiful design. When sin entered creation and marred us and our environment, it demanded a primary place in our focus through feelings of guilt and shame. Because of this, many Christians spend their lives rummaging around in their soul trying to root out every evidence of sin. This level of self-focus does not lead to life, but rather despair. Scripture instead calls us to yes, put our sin to death, but even more so to keep our attention on Christ and run toward His righteousness.

IN SESSION COUNSELING
Read Romans 6:12–14 and 2 Timothy 2:22.

What do these passages call us to do?
- Run and pursue righteousness. This is not a passive endeavor. This is an effortful call as was Joseph choosing to run naked from Potiphar's wife to avoid the snares of sin and temptation.
- We are to fight against sin's attempts to rule in our lives. Before Christ we were slaves to sin, but in Christ we are set free and sin's dominion in our lives is fundamentally broken. We need to practice living free from sin's ruling reign in our lives.
- We are to do this life in community with others who love and are pursuing righteousness as well. We are not called to do this alone, but rather with the help of the body of Christ.

What keeps us from running after Christ?
- Shame and guilt. If we give all our attention to the totality of sin in our lives it can overwhelm us and leave us in despair. When sin is central in our focus, we will feel hopeless.
- Weariness. We have fought the good fight for a season, but now we feel tired and faint- hearted. We need encouragement and support but find ourselves unwilling to ask for help (Hebrews 3:13). We have fallen prey to the false belief that *I can do this on my own.*
- We misunderstand repentance, thinking it only means identifying and putting to death our sin. We fail to realize that repentance is more than just saying we will stop doing bad things, but rather is only complete when we have turned from our sin toward Christ and His righteousness. Yes, we put sin to death, but even more we run toward righteousness in Christ.

Run toward righteousness:
- We are called to run after Christ our forerunner and the perfector of our faith (Hebrews 12:1-2). Our life is about Him and knowing Him above all else, and in that process learning who He has made us to be and how He has made us to live.
- What helps you run toward righteousness? What in life helps you keep your eyes on Christ?
- What is slowing you down in running toward righteousness? What do you need to let go of to be able to move forward?

AFTER SESSION ASSIGNMENT

1. When tempted, do you flee from sin? Why or why not?

2. Do some self-analysis: Do you spend more time focused on your sin or on what Christ has done? Do you find yourself spending more effort on finding sin in your life or running after righteousness?

3. Do you have a community surrounding you as you run toward Christ? If not, why? Pray that God would surround you with fellow brothers and sisters who will encourage you to keep running and that He would help you to encourage others as they run the race of life well. Ask God to bring to mind people you could ask to help you in pursuing righteousness.

4. What practical steps can you take today to grow your habit of pursuing righteousness?

2 CORINTHIANS 5

16-17

TRULY SEEING OURSELVES

By: Andrew Dealy

www.AustinStoneCounseling.org

2 CORINTHIANS 5:16-17

How do you define who you are? Your answer to this question will set the parameters of what you think you are able to do. If your definition of self is composed of your past failures and successes, your future options will be bound by those experiences. God offers us a better way to view ourselves. In fact, instead of us defining ourselves, He invites us to let Him tell us who we are and what we can do.

IN SESSION COUNSELING

Read 2 Corinthians 5:16–17 together and discuss the following questions.

What does it mean to regard someone according to the flesh?
- When we regard ourselves according to the flesh, we judge based on what we can see. We shape our identity around our perception of what we do and don't do.
- Assess your self-identity: What most influences your view of yourself? Are you more informed by what God says about you or what you say about yourself?

What is the danger of regarding someone according to the flesh?
- Our perception of ourselves is always incomplete. We only see a part of who we are, and making judgments based on partial knowledge is naturally faulty. This inevitably leads to us limiting our belief of what we are capable of based on what we see in our lives.
- 2 Corinthians 4:17–18 reminds us that the unseen is eternal, but the seen is transient. We are invited to focus more on what is unseen than what is seen, but we often get this backward. It's difficult to see past the faults in our lives and embrace the greater truths of what God has declared about us.

What does it mean to be a new creation?
- Your old self has been buried with Christ. Your sin has been paid for. When you live like your old self, you are now living contrary to who God has declared you to be. Our sin does not have the power to change our identity any longer because of what Christ has done on our behalf.
- We are invited to look more at Christ and less at ourselves. He defines who we are. He has made us new. We are presently learning to walk in the newness of life that He has already given us (Hebrews 10:14).
- Christ sets the parameters for what we can and cannot do. We are invited to live in joy- filled faith recognizing that our weaknesses and struggles do not determine what Christ can do in and through us. He lovingly sets our limits.

AFTER SESSION ASSIGNMENT

1. In what ways has regarding yourself according to the flesh limited what you believe you can do? Ask God to help you see this clearly and then ask Him to help you see what He is calling you to do.

2. Your old self is buried with Christ. How will this truth shape the way you live today?

3. You are a new creation. What practices and habits can you put into place to help remind yourself of who God says you are?

4. **Considering others:** Ask God to reveal any relationships in which you are regarding the other person according to the flesh. Pray that He will give you the ability to see them as He does and to respond to them as He would. Ask for courage to repent and the ability to love the other person as a fellow child of God.

NOTES

GALATIANS 5 1-4

STANDING FIRM IN FREEDOM

By: Jeremy Lelek

www.ChristianCounseling.com

What comes to mind when you consider the idea of freedom in counseling? As a believer do you consider freedom a state of being or a targeted outcome? Is freedom an already reality or is it a goal to pursue? One could answer in the affirmative to both, but for the saint only one of these actually captures the essence of the Gospel. This passage is intended to help believers embrace the beauty of freedom as realized in the finished work of Jesus alone.

IN SESSION COUNSELING

Read Galatians 5:1

Based on this passage, what is Paul referring to when he encourages Christians to stand firm in their freedom? Is it freedom from the struggle with sin, freedom from negative emotions, freedom to be obedient or something else?

What is Paul referring to when he mentions the "yoke of slavery"? Is the yoke of slavery one's former bondage to sin or something else?

Read Galatians 5:2

Circumcision equals the law. Is this perhaps what Paul is referring to when he mentions the yoke of slavery? How does this inform the process of change? How does relying on outcome or performance impact our experience of the Gospel according to this passage?

Read Galatians 5:3–4

What happens when a person relies on his or her performance (and outcome) in counseling as the basis of freedom?

How does Paul conceptualize the idea of "falling from grace" here?

What severs believers from experiencing the abundance of the Gospel?

AFTER SESSION ASSIGNMENT

Read the following passages and list the freedoms and abundance you possess in your union with Jesus:

Romans 6:14	Hebrews 4:14–16
Romans 8:1–2	Hebrews 10:11–18
Colossians 3:3	Titus 2:11–14

Pray a prayer of earnest gratitude for what the Lord provides you in the Gospel in your pursuit of change.

EPHESIANS 4

31-32

RENEWED ATTITUDES & BEHAVIORS

By: Dr. Ray Hicks

www.sv.church

In this passage, the Apostle Paul tells us of six self-focused behavioral words that we need to offload from our hearts and minds. Then Paul gives us three Christ-centered, Gospel-focused, active-heart, relationship-enhancing words for us to upload and make active parts of our daily lives.

The six self-centered behavioral words to offload from our hearts will always create bitterness in the relationships with those in our lives or with our spouse. They are behaviors that destroy relationships. And, finally, these six self-centered behaviors create distance between us and those in our lives.

The three attitudes of the heart behavior-words to upload are "kind, tender-hearted, and forgiving." These three Christ-centered attitudes of the heart give life, grace, encouragement, and hope to those in our lives with whom we show these attitudes.

IN SESSION COUNSELING

Take two sessions to unpack the two verses in Ephesians 4:31–32. In each session begin by reading the Scripture passage and then walk through the following points.

The goal of the first session will be to uncover the six relationship-crushing behaviors from the counselee's heart and mind. Define each of the behavioral-attitudes with your counselee and then help them confessionally unpack their heart toward others and the impact on their relationship. Examine other biblical passages that focus on these sin-filled behaviors. (James 1:19–20; Ephesians 4:26; Psalm 37:8; James 1:20; and Hebrews 12:15)

- **Bitterness:** This is unprocessed anger, pain, and brokenness in one's life; and the toxins of those spill into the lives of others or one's spouse.
- **Anger:** This is fierce indignation that hurts and cuts the heart of another.
- **Wrath:** This is the violent, vengeful, or punishing anger that wants to hurt another person emotionally or physically.
- **Shouting:** This is screaming or shouting with the intent to hurt or get your own way over another.
- **Slander:** This is speaking evil or hurtfully toward another. It also includes cursing at someone to damage their heart.
- **Malice:** This is evil and wickedness purposefully mean to hurt another.

The goal of the second session will be to upload the three grace-filled behaviors of being kind, tender-hearted, and forgiving. These will offer hope, health, and healing in the counselee's relationships with their spouse and/or with others. Define each of the behavioral-attitudes with your counselee and then process practical ways they can start living this out within their relationships.

- **Kind:** means to be gracious. It requires that the person has received God's grace in salvation and extends it to others. Being kind is a tangible action that results from compassion.

- **Compassionate:** means to be "tender-hearted." Having a tender-hearted attitude means that you express a heartfelt sympathy or empathy toward others. This comes from what we have experienced in God's tenderness ourselves by His rescue when we stumble, sin, or fail.
- **Forgiving:** means to graciously pardon or rescue. We can be forgiving because we have been recipients of His forgiveness for our sins. That forgiveness enables us to forgive others and/or our spouse.

AFTER SESSION ASSIGNMENT

The main focus of the assignment is to develop the three key attitudes and behaviors of kindness, compassionate tender-heartedness, and forgiveness.

1. Do a word-study on each of the three grace-filled words. You can use the free software blueletterbible.com.

2. Make a list of the relationships in your life and how you could use these grace-filled words, behaviors, and attitudes in each of your relationships.

3. Pray each day that God will help to offload the negative attitudes and upload the Christ-centered attitudes of the heart that will honor the Lord and the relationships in your life.

4. Journal as you process these within your relationships so we can discuss together in our next session.

NOTES

PHILIPPIANS 2 1-8

WINNING THE POWER STRUGGLE IN MARRIAGE

By: Jeremy Lelek
www.speakthetruth.org

Very often couples experience strife and division in their marriages because they become embroiled in bitter, exhausting power struggles. Each spouse one-upping the other tends to create a dynamic where escalation, tension, and anger flourish. The endgame to such relational interactions will inevitably produce a marriage characterized by resentment, emptiness, and a divided home—something Jesus warned cannot stand (Mark 3:25). This passage provides a Christ-centered alternative to help couples break out of sinful, harmful power struggles while growing in the likeness of Jesus within their marriage.

IN SESSION COUNSELING

1. Ask each spouse to define his or her understanding of power in marriage. Maybe ask each to explain what they understand as being a "power struggle."

2. Ask for examples of what individuals may do to win power struggles in marriage. Ask the couple to self-reflect and consider where they may be engaging in a power struggle. How might this be impacting the relationship?

3. Read Philippians 2:1–4 and discuss what these passages mention that might characterize a godly, loving marriage?

4. Read Philippians 2:5–8 and have the couple highlight the five things Jesus did in these passages that brought forth the possibility of restoration between God and humanity (a relationship fractured by the prideful attempt to power grab by Adam and Eve).

   • He did not count equality with God a thing to be grasped—he didn't fight for what was rightfully his own.
   • He made himself nothing.
   • He took the form of a servant.
   • He humbled himself.
   • He was obedient to the point of death.

5. These are what reflect godly, God-centered power in relationships. Have the couple discuss these ideas within the session. Do they resonate? Are they challenged? Do they agree? Why/why not?

6. Work with the couple through each item listed above, and help them formulate ideas to practically reflect these in their marriage. Jot these down to hand to the couple at the conclusion of the session.

PHILIPPIANS 2:1-8

AFTER SESSION ASSIGNMENT

1. Reflect and build upon the practical applications from Philippians 2:5–8

2. Journal the joys and challenges of implementing these practical ideas throughout the week. Bring journals to the next session to process.

3. Read and meditate on 2 Peter 1:3–4 then consider how these verses apply to implementing divine, Christ-reflecting power within their marriage.

HEBREWS 3

12–13

ENCOURAGEMENT IN RELATIONSHIPS

By: Dr. Ray Hicks

www.sv.church

HEBREWS 3:12-13

This passage in Hebrews gives believers a relationship command to encourage. It is a daily imperative (command) that if we neglect, we face the real possibility of being hardened by the deceitfulness and deceptiveness of sin.

IN SESSION COUNSELING

Ask your counselee to read Hebrews 3:12–13 aloud and discuss the following questions together. Help them unpack what encouragement is and reflect how that is offered in their current relationships.

How would they define encourage?
* The word "encourage" in Greek is *parakaleo*, which is made up of two words–para meaning "alongside," and *kaleo* meaning to "call out or shout out courage." So, to encourage means "to come alongside someone and shout out words of courage to them."

How do you encourage people in your relationships? Is it more about thanking them for what they do, than for who they are in your life?
* In John 14:26 the Greek word for Comforter is *parakletos*. It is from the same root word as "encourage." It means intercessor, consoler, advocate, and comforter. Those four words are what happen when we encourage one another.

What hinders your counselee from encouraging others? Do they struggle in specific relationships? Do these struggles concern their spouse, friends, kids, parents, church family, co-workers?
* Encouragement is a healthy step toward improving relationships. The counselee must remember that encouragement is about affirming, valuing, and honoring the person about not only what they do, but also who they are. This isn't about what the person is or isn't doing for us, but our call to encourage others.

How have you been hardened by the deceitfulness of sin because of your lack of encouraging others?
* 1 John 1:9 says that "if we confess our sins, he is faithful and just to forgive us our sins and to cleanse us from all unrighteousness."

How can you make Hebrews 3:12–13 an active part of the relationships in your life?
* If encouraging becomes an active part of your daily life, you will find you will be encouraged by how it affects your relationships. And, you will find that those you encourage will find themselves encouraging you too.

AFTER SESSION ASSIGNMENT

The focus of this assignment is to show that encouragement is an important command within our relationships. Without it, the deceitfulness of sin will creep into those relationships and cause cracks in them.

1. Make a list of ways you can encourage the closest people in your life. Then, begin to carry out the love-motivated encouragement of those relationships.

2. Make a list of how you might encourage the most difficult people in your life. Then, begin the faith journey of encouraging them.

3. Make a list of how you can encourage your spouse. Now, step out in Christ and begin encouraging him/her.

HEBREWS 5₇

BIBLICAL EXPRESSION OF SORROW

By: Curtis Solomon

www.solomonsoulcare.com • www.biblicalcc.org

Many people, including Christians, don't know what to do with sadness. We don't like being sad. We don't like being around people who are sad. Sometimes we aren't even sure it's okay to be sad. While few people will come straight out and say, "Sadness is a sin," we often think along those lines. We think that loving God and having good theology should mean that we don't experience sadness, especially not deep or long-lasting sorrow. If we do experience sorrow we think that our belief in God's sovereignty and goodness should help us get over that sorrow quickly. However, the life of Jesus gives us a very different understanding of our encounters with sorrow. This study is a great comfort to those who are wrestling with illegitimate shame related to the sadness they experience in life.

IN SESSION COUNSELING
Read Hebrews 5:7 and discuss the following questions and ideas.

How would you describe the emotional experience of Jesus in this passage?

- Allow time for them to ponder the question and then encourage a fully articulated answer. If they offer a short response prompt them for further thoughts.

Would you say He is a little sad, expressing a medium amount of sorrow, or expressing deep sadness?

- The language used here by the author of Hebrews points to a deeply stirring and painful emotional experience. Jesus is not unmoved emotionally. He doesn't simply speak to God in His prayer, but calls out with "loud cries and tears."

When did this happen in Jesus' life?

- "In the days of his flesh," describes when Jesus experienced such deep sorrow. The Gospels recount the earthly ministry of Jesus and there we find one very clear event that would certainly fit with this emotional stirring, Jesus' prayer in the Garden of Gethsemane (Matthew 26:36–46, Mark 14:32–42, Luke 22:39–46). But there are other passages that describe Jesus expressing deep sorrow as well (John 11:35, Luke 19:41). When we broaden our eyes to take in the whole counsel of God we see Jesus described in Isaiah 53:3 as a "a man of sorrows and acquainted with grief." The Jesus of the Bible felt and expressed deep sadness.

Use the following rhetorical questions to draw out and emphasize common false beliefs about sorrow: Did Jesus have good theology? Did Jesus trust God and His goodness? Did Jesus understand that His death on the cross was part of God's plan and would bring about good?

- The obvious "no" answer to these questions points out the falsehood of the accusations we often make against ourselves and others.

What does that teach us about whether sadness and sorrow are necessarily sinful?

- Jesus, being God, is sinless. Anything He does is without sin. Therefore, sadness and expressions of deep sorrow cannot be sinful. Of course, sin can be intermingled with our sadness, but the mere existence of deep sorrow is not evidence of sin. We should not jump to conclusions but investigate thoroughly the heart of our counselee to help them identify and turn from sin. But we also need to help them to appropriately grieve the losses they experience in life.

Who does Jesus address in this verse?

- Jesus calls out with "loud cries and tears, to him who was able to save him from death." Jesus cries out to our Heavenly Father in the midst of His pain and suffering. Seasons of suffering can tempt us to question God, to doubt, Him, to accuse Him, and to draw away from Him. The example Jesus sets for us, as well as many other sufferers in Scripture, is to move toward God. We should cast our cares on Him (1 Peter 5:7) in lament, honestly baring our souls to Him in communion with Him. He truly understands our suffering (Hebrews 4:15).

What does all this teach us about our own experience of sadness?

- We should be encouraged to see that sadness is not sinful but a normal part of the human experience in this fallen world. Our goal, emotionally, is not the avoidance of negative emotions and to only experience positive ones. The goal is to emote the way God would emote. If something would make God grieve, then we should likewise grieve. If God would rejoice over something, then rejoicing should be our emotional state as well. When we encounter something that is sad, we should freely express our sorrow. We should go to God with our concerns, our sadness, and our confusion and cry out to Him.

AFTER SESSION ASSIGNMENT

1. Read Matthew 26:36–46. How would you describe Jesus' emotional experience?

2. Read Psalm 73 and Psalm 88. What kinds of emotions are expressed in these psalms? How did they make you feel? Who were the writers of the psalms talking to?

3. How has this study informed your own emotional experience and expression?

4. Take some time and write your own psalm of lament to God. Think of a specific loss you have experienced and write to God about how it made you feel and what you thought/think about it. List any questions or concerns you still have regarding that situation. Then sit with Him in silence for a while.

If you want to learn more about biblical expressions of sorrow and lament or need guidance on writing a psalm of lament, see *Dark Clouds Deep Mercy* by Mark Vroegop, or *God's Healing for Life's Losses* by Robert Kellemen.

HEBREWS 6

17–20

ANCHOR OF THE SOUL

By: Shanda Anderson
www.AustinStoneCounseling.org

Hebrews 6:17–20 offers hope to those who are suffering and discouraged. This offer of refuge implies that those who are called by God will struggle and need to find shelter throughout their journey of faith. We are reminded that our hope is anchored in heaven because Jesus has gone before us to secure our confidence in God's love. Because Christ lived in perfect obedience and died the death that we deserved, we now look to Him and know that His finished work on the cross provides confidence that we will enter into glory with Him. Jesus enables us to hope because He guarantees our future eternal inheritance. Your subjective hoping is anchored in an objective hope in the One who offered Himself that you might have freedom and abundant life, even in the midst of sorrow and suffering.

IN SESSION COUNSELING
Read Hebrew 6:17–20 and discuss the following points.

Point 1: God's unchangeable purpose and pledge (v. 17)
- As Jesus "showed" his nail-scarred hands and feet to Thomas, offering proof to the doubts that hindered the disciple to believe that Jesus had been resurrected, God "shows" and reminds those He calls of their secure and steadfast hope. All that God requires, His benevolent grace provides through Christ. God's plan to redeem sinners is accomplished, completed, and guaranteed for those who confess Christ as Lord and Savior. (Romans 10:9)
- You can have assurance of your eternal destination when you hope in, hide in, rely on, put your faith in, and surrender to Christ, your perfect Advocate. He is your confidence and guarantee. Boast only in Him. What fears and discouragements tempt you to doubt that your hope is secure?

Point 2: We who have fled for refuge have strong encouragement (v. 18a)
- In the Old Testament there were cities of refuge where those fearing danger would run to find shelter and safety. Christ is our sanctuary and safe harbor where we now run to find covering and shade from the perils of this dark and dangerous world.
- Christ invites us to shelter in His wounds and attach our life to Him as we face life's storms. Where do you often run to find refuge other than Christ?

Point 3: Hold fast to the hope set before us… a sure and steadfast anchor of the soul (v. 18b–20)
- Your ability to hold on to Jesus is not what offers you security. Having faith in Christ unites you to Him and binds you to Him. Holding fast to Him is the evidence and proof of you exchanging your imperfect strength for His perfect strength. Lay down your feeble efforts and anchor yourself to Him. Where are you resisting and hesitating to release your grasp on something or someone you are looking to for hope and security?
- In Hebrews 12:1–3 we see Jesus enduring the cross for the hope set before Him. Here in Hebrews 6:18, we are called to follow His example and remember His willing surrender and obedience when we face difficult times. There is always eternal hope available and in every circumstance. How does this truth impact you today?

AFTER SESSION ASSIGNMENT

"God has given strong encouragement, even in difficult times, to rejoice in the Lord though every nerve should twinge, and every bone should seem melted into jelly with pain." C. H. Spurgeon

1. Read John 16:33 and 1 Peter 4:12. Spend time journaling your thoughts and feelings as you respond to the Spurgeon quote and these scriptures.

2. What is the Spirit illuminating as you contemplate these ideas?

3. What practical application might you be able to implement in your life in light of these verses?

For further study, read Psalm 42 and 43 and "Strong Consolation" No. 893 by C.H. Spurgeon.

NOTES

HEBREWS12
1-2

LOCKING OUR EYES & HEART ON JESUS

By: Dr. Ray Hicks

www.sv.church

This biblical narrative is speaking to those who are struggling with life's issues and with sin in their lives and in the church. In our lives as believers, we have so many who form a "great cloud of witnesses" to the Gospel-power of Christ in our lives, the presence of the Holy Spirit, and the changed lives of believers in Christ who are witnesses to His transforming power in their lives.

This transformational testimony of believers gives us courage to stand against the sin that can ensnare us if we do not stand strong and walk in Christ daily. So, not only do we have the witness of believers around us, but the writer encourages us to "run with endurance the race that lies before us." How do we do that? The writer tells us that the key to dealing with the "hindrances" of life and the sin that we battle with daily is to "fix our eyes on Jesus, the pioneer, and perfecter of our faith."

The word "hindrance" has to do with the weight or load of our struggles that burden down our lives. The "sin" are those self-centered sins, faults, and trespasses that cause us to miss the mark in our walk with Christ. The phrase "keeping our eyes on Jesus" is such a beautiful word picture. It is certainly a fixing of our attention and our hearts on the One who is the Author and Finisher of our faith.

Life is to be all about Him, no matter what we are struggling with. No matter how broken we are. No matter how fractured the relationships of our lives are. No matter how hopeless our marriage has become. Before we address any of these things and before we deal with the hurts and struggles of our lives, and before we can battle the sin of our hearts, OUR EYES MUST BE FIXED ON JESUS!

This biblical narrative will help the counselee get things in line in their relationship with the Lord before they begin addressing the struggles and sins of their lives, relationships, and/or marriage.

IN SESSION COUNSELING

If this is a new counselee, start with #1. If this is an existing counselee then you might start with #4 based off what you have already gathered in previous sessions.

1. Have the counselee describe what brought them into counseling.

2. Help the counselee determine areas they are struggling in. (Make a list on the glass board.)

3. Help the counselee discern areas of sin in their life.

4. Help the counselee discuss what relationships in their lives have been affected by the areas above.

5. Then, lay numbers 1–4 aside and help them grasp what "fixing or keeping their eyes on Jesus" means by walking them through Hebrews 12:1–2.

6. If ready, guide them through the steps of confession, repentance, and forgiveness with the Lord so they can begin to "fix their eyes on Jesus."

AFTER SESSION ASSIGNMENT
The goal is to help you learn how to daily "fix your eyes on Jesus."

1. Memorize Hebrews 12:1–2.

2. The letter to the Hebrews is a total of 13 chapters. Read two chapters a day and then one chapter on the last day. Take notes and highlight the areas that stand out.

3. Reflect on these three questions after each daily reading and write a summary:
   • What is God teaching me about Him?
   • What is God teaching me about me?
   • What changes does God want me to make in my life so that my eyes stay fixed on Him?

4. Bring your Bible and summaries to our next session so we can discuss together.

NOTES

HEBREWS 12
1-3

RUN WITH ENDURANCE

By: Shanda Anderson
www.AustinStoneCounseling.org

Hebrews 12:1–3 should be considered as a response to Hebrews 11 where Noah, Abraham, Jacob, Sarah, and several other people from the Old Testament are remembered for their faith that remained strong through trials and challenging circumstances. As Christians, we are called to "run with endurance" because we will, like those mentioned in Hebrews 11, face many obstacles and bump up against the brokenness in this sin-sick world. We will wage battles with our own flesh and we will wrestle with our feeble hearts so prone to wander. We will suffer great disappointments and discouragements in relationships where we get hurt and we also hurt others. Without looking to Jesus for our ultimate hope and confidence, the suffering and temptations common to all mankind will extinguish our hope and joy. Only Christ and His finished work on the cross can sustain the weary traveler and guard against our instincts to give up and doubt the love and goodness of God. Christ is our perfect model of enduring the unwanted path of pain, and He now sits in the seat of honor at God's right hand and prays for us to not give up and exchange the glory of God for the things of this world.

IN SESSION COUNSELING
Read Hebrews 12:1-3 and discuss the following points.

Point 1: Who is cheering you on and what is weighing you down? v. 1
- The examples of faith from Hebrews 11 offer testimonies of keeping an eternal perspective in the midst of earthly trials. Let the stories of their faith cheer you on and remind you that the cost of following Jesus is worthy of your life. Who in your life encourages you to persevere through dark and difficult times?
- Unconfessed sin, hidden patterns of disobedience, and unforgiveness will hinder your daily worship and intimate fellowship with Christ. Is there anything you need to talk to God or someone in your life about in order to bring any unresolved issues to the light? If so, be bold and courageous and repent so that you can live in redemptive freedom.
- In this passage we are compelled to think of journeying with Jesus as a marathon instead of a sprint, the long haul that requires is intentional choosing to start with the end in mind. Jesus ran the race perfectly on our behalf; and now, by faith in Him, we just keep putting one foot in front of the other until we cross the finish line. Be encouraged and keep running. The eternal rewards of imperishable riches await you. (Timothy 4:7–8)

Point 2: Where are you focusing your mind and fixing your eyes? v. 2
- Futile and temporal things of this world can easily capture our attention and affections. The Greek word for "fix" or "look to" in verse 2 means "to look away from or turn from other things." What takes up mental real estate in your mind and preoccupies your thought life that leads you away from Jesus?
- There is a saying, "You become what you behold." What changes in your life can you make to "behold" more of Christ and become more like Him?

Point 3: You have good reason to hope and endure in faith. v. 3
- The word "endure" shows up in all three verses. It means to stay under, remain, continue in, have fortitude, or abide patiently. We are called to endure because Christ has endured on our behalf. How does remembering and considering the truth that Christ faced the ultimate hardships and sufferings by 1) dying the death we deserved, 2) being raised from the dead, 3) ascending into Heaven, and 4) now sitting at the right hand of God impact the way you think about the trials you are now facing? How does it help you endure and not grow weary? Where are you tempted to grow weary and lose heart?

AFTER SESSION ASSIGNMENT

1. Read Hebrews 11:24–28 and compare with Hebrews 12:1–3. What similarities do you notice? How does this story of Moses living out his faith and persevering through trials encourage you? Where in your life can you consider Christ of greater value than the treasures of this world and resist "enjoying the fleeting pleasures of sin"?

2. Read Philippians 4:7–9 and Colossians 3:1–3. List the things that are offered for you to "think about" and "set your mind on." Throughout the day look at the list you made and practice turning your attention toward these truths. Continue meditating on and rehearsing these truths throughout the week until they become familiar friends and helpful companions to you during times of distress.

3. Read Galatians 6:9 and Philippians 1:6. Reflect on these verses, journal honestly about the areas of life where you are weary, and ponder the motivation offered in these verses to have hope that God is with you and for you. If you feel comfortable, share with a friend who will pray for you about the difficulties you are facing.

JAMES 4

DESTRUCTIVE DESIRES & THE GRACE OF GOD

By: John Henderson
www.ChristianCounseling.com

JAMES 4

"I the Lord search the heart and test the mind…" (Jeremiah 17:10) God sees. God hears. God knows. God understands. And, hallelujah, God tells! James 4 is one of those passages where God tells us what He sees. God peels back the layers of our thinking and feeling and behaving, peels back the layers of our attitudes and activities and relationships and says: "Here's the big danger in your life! Here's your most serious problem!" Yes, you are afflicted. Yes, you are mistreated. Yes, there are many things that go wrong, but here is the reality that will destroy your soul and your relationships and your life. *Do we want to know?*

IN SESSION COUNSELING

Read James 4:1–10 and guide your counselee through the points below to gain the overall takeaway - *Proud, sinful desires are the greatest dangers to our souls, for they wage war against God and others. Our greatest hope is the grace of God in Christ, and our greatest task is to humble ourselves before God in repentance and faith.*

The greatest problem is our proud desires.

What causes quarrels and fights among you? What causes suffering in our life? They are all true sources of pain and affliction and suffering and trouble. They are not, however, good answers to the question: "What causes us to fight? What causes us to quarrel? What causes our attitudes? What causes our behavior? The causes of our suffering are not the same as the cause of us. Understanding the difference between the two is massively important. It will make the difference between:

- A life of hardened un-repentance and a life of humble repentance
- A life of ever-deepening despair and a life of unshakable hope
- A life of joyful gratitude or a life of constant blame and grumbling
- A life enslaved to people and circumstances or a life free to enjoy God under all circumstances
- A life of conflict and frustration or a life of peace and contentment
- A life stuck in the mud of failures and disappointments or a life of Christ-centered transformation

Our desires: *Is it not this: that your passions are at war within you? You desire and do not have, so you murder. You covet and cannot obtain, so you fight and quarrel.* That's what causes us to get frustrated, angry, and bitter. The primary problem is inside us, not outside us. Our passions for money, for power, for pleasure, for being right, for safety, for approval, for possessions, for honor, for ease, for well-behaved children, for a spouse or for certain kind of spouse, for better roommates, for better politicians, for better drivers on the road, for less traffic, for respect, for a thousand other things. *I war* because *I want*. We desire money and possessions, the Lord puts people into our lives who get in the way of our money and possessions, and we go to war. We crave approval, and the Lord carefully brings disapproving people from every direction. We crave respect, and the Lord brings disrespect out of nowhere. He withholds things as basic as food and water to show us who we really trust and what we really worship. The circumstances don't cause us to sin. They expose our sin.

Our pride: *God opposes the proud*, even His own children who would continue to live as the self-appointed sovereigns of their personal kingdoms. Pride is my greatest danger. Pride sets me against God. Pride destroys my soul. Pride compels my warring with others. I'm proud. That's my problem. Do you believe this to be true about your heart and life? Pride is the chief cause of your misery. People can hurt you, but they're not the reason you're an idol worshipper. Circumstances can be painful, but circumstances aren't the reason you love the world. People and circumstances don't harm your soul. Pride does. Pride is the mother of all your sins, and mine. It is the cancer that kills our relationship to God and one another.

The greater hope is God's grace.

God opposes the proud, but gives grace to the humble. Not merely grace, but more grace. The whole passage turns on verse 6. It is the beam of sunlight through the storm clouds. However deep our selfishness may run, however wide our sinful desires flow, for however long our idolatry has persisted, the God of all grace promises more grace. The cure for our conflicts and quarrels is God's grace. We don't need a new job. We don't need new cars, houses, and possessions. We don't need a spouse or a child. We don't need a different spouse or a different child. We don't need better parents, or better weather, or better schooling, or better health. These are all marvelous gifts and provisions from the Lord if He desires to give them. What we need more than anything is the reconciling and transforming grace of God.

The great task of humility, repentance, and faith.

What James says in verses 7–10 is both convicting and freeing: *convicting* in that his words place the responsibility for everything that comes from us upon us: all our desires and all the mayhem our desires bring upon our relationships. Yet his words are *freeing* because they focus our attention squarely upon our hearts before God, rather than everyone else. The Lord does not ask us to change the world. He does not ask us to fix everyone else. We can pray for others. We can encourage others. Sometimes we can reprove others. At all times we bear patiently with others. But above all things, we must strive to be humble and repentant with our own proud desires. We must learn to trust God with the entirety of our lives.

Action 1: Rather than exerting all our energy quarreling and fighting, we have been assigned a simple and vital task: be humble, which means,
- Verse 7: *Submit yourselves therefore to God*, rather than selfish passions and self-serving actions,
- Verse 7: *Resist the devil*, rather than act as his servant with murderous attitudes. Don't yield to his temptations, which comes with a promise: and *he will flee from you.*
- Verse 8: *Draw near to God*, by crying out in prayer and feasting upon His Word and banking upon His promises and adoring Christ as Savior and revering Christ as Lord and being satisfied in His love and seeking first His kingdom and holding to the things of the world loosely and being content in His provision, which comes with another promise: *and he will draw near to you.*

God looking to us with favor is far more glorious than winning arguments. Better to tremble before Him as an unworthy recipient of grace than stomp into His presence with grumbling and complaining. Better to live grateful than entitled. Better to serve, than be served. Rather than smuggling our idolatrous desires around as "needs," and "prayer requests," and "endless hurt feelings," we must, by God's grace, bring our idols into the light and ask God to pound them into the dust, which is where James takes us next.

Action 2: Rather than exerting all our energy defending ourselves and justifying our sin, we learn to see our sin as sin and turn from it to Christ. Rather than trying to worship Christ and the world at the same time (*"double-minded"*), we worship Christ alone, which means we'll hold created things loosely. Rather than mourning and weeping about not getting what we want, we mourn and weep for how wrongly we want what we want. *Cleanse your hands, you sinners, and purify your hearts, you double-minded. Be wretched and mourn and weep. Let your laughter be turned to mourning and your joy to gloom (v8b-9).* This is the language of repentance.

Action 3: Rather than exerting all our energy pursuing the world and the things of the world, we must exert ourselves in pursuit of greater faith. James again counsels us: *Humble yourselves before the Lord, and he will exalt you (v10).* The final expression of humility in the passage is trusting that God will exalt us at the proper time. Faith trusts in God's timing, means, and provision. Pride trusts in our timing, means, and provision.
- Pride is self-exalting. Humble faith is self-lowering, trusting in the Lord to exalt us at the proper time.
- Pride is ambitious. Humble faith is content, trusting in the sufficient grace of God as He provides for us.
- Pride is self-centered. Humble faith is self-forgetting, trusting in the Lord to remember us when the time comes.
- Pride is self-protective. Humble faith is self-sacrificing, trusting in the Lord to care for us in His way.

Without God's grace, we're in trouble. Without repentance, we waste away. Without humility, we burn everything that matters to the ground. Without faith, it's impossible to please God. The gospel frees us from sinful desires to focus upon what truly and eternally matters: God, His glory, His promises, and life everlasting with all the saints in a place where worldly worries are no more. Lord, help us believe and obey!

AFTER SESSION ASSIGNMENT

1. When you consider what angers you, even what your quarrel is over, even quietly in your heart, the grumbling and complaining, what do you prize more than Christ? Where is your treasure?

2. Do you love money more than God? Safety? Human praise? Sex? Power? Respect? Pleasure? Comfort? Reputation? What do you fight over?

3. Do I want more of God, or more of the world? Do I want my passions, or do I want grace? Will I fear the loss of stuff, or will I fear the loss of God? Read Isaiah 66:1–2.

4. Go back through our session notes and read James 4 again. What changes are needed in your heart and life? Pray without ceasing that the Lord helps you to believe and obey. Thank the Lord for his abounding grace (Romans 6).

1 PETER 5

5-10

SUBMISSION IN SUFFERING

By: Michael Van Dyke
www.TruthRenewed.org

Peter's first epistle addresses two realities living as God's people; the implications of our salvation and our suffering.[1] In the first-century, when this epistle was written, Christian persecution was inevitable. It was experienced at varying degrees in various places.[2] Suffering and persecution, which are realities for every generation in Christ,[3] are best understood in the context of spiritual warfare. As Christians, we battle against three warring entities: the world, our flesh, and the devil.[4]

IN SESSION COUNSELING

Read 1 Peter 5:5–10 aloud. Discuss the commands given in these verses and discuss how they apply in daily life.

Verse 5: Peter provides two imperatives in this verse, "subject" and "clothe." Exclusively, he is addressing the younger brothers' demeanor in the presence of their elders. And secondly, more inclusively, he's addressing everyone in the church[5] and commands them to clothe themselves with humility toward one another. It's in this context that Peter quotes James 4:6 and Proverbs 3:34, saying, "God opposes the proud but gives grace to the humble," suggesting that if we don't clothe ourselves with humility toward one another, we're being prideful and in opposition to God.

- What do you think it means to be "subject" to someone and to "clothe" yourself with humility toward one another?
- Provide a biblical definition to correct any inconsistencies in their thinking:
  – Subject (to be submissive) = to be or become inclined or willing to submit to orders or wishes of others.
  – Clothe with humility = to put on the disposition of valuing or assessing oneself appropriately; especially considering one's sinfulness and creatureliness.
- What relationships are you struggling to submit to and to demonstrate humility in all of them?
- Where do you think pride is involved?

Verse 6: The imperative in this verse is to "humble" yourselves. Under whom? God. And at the proper time, He will exalt you.

- What do you think it means to humble yourself under God's mighty hand?
- What do you think it means that God will exalt you?
- Provide a biblical definition to correct any inconsistencies in their thinking:
  – Humble (to be brought low) = to be or become reduced in rank, character, or status.
  – Exalt (raise up) = to exalt someone, conceived of as lifting the person up.

---

[1] 1 Peter 1:3-5:11
[2] 1 Peter 1:6; 4:12; 5:9; James 1:2
[3] 2 Timothy 3:12
[4] Ephesians 2:1-3; 1 John 2:15-16; 1 Peter 5:8
[5] 1 Peter 2:5

Verse 7: Because God cares for you, he said to cast our anxieties onto him. So, we submit our worries to God and trust in Him.

- Do you cast your anxieties on God? How can you begin doing that?

Verse 8: There are two imperatives in this verse, sober-minded and watchful. Why? Because your adversary, the devil is always seeking to destroy someone.

- What do you think it means to be sober-minded and watchful?
- Provide a biblical definition to correct any inconsistencies in their thinking:
  - Sober minded (self-control) = to curb the controlling influence of inordinate emotions or desires (and therefore become reasonable)
  - Watchful (be alert) = to be awake

Verse 9: Peter gives his last imperative in this section, to "resist" the devil. How? By trusting in the person and work of Christ and trusting the testimony of the scriptures that explicitly teach that we will suffer, but we will also experience, eternally, the glories of Christ (Rom. 8:18; 2 Cor. 4:17; 1 Pet. 1:5–9; 5:10).

- How would you define "resist"?
- How do you understand faith?
- Provide a biblical definition to correct any inconsistencies in their thinking:
  - Resist (oppose) = to be against, express opposition to.
  - Faith = trust in the gospel (person and work of Christ)

Verse 10: Peter didn't say, if you suffer, but after you've suffered a little while, God will restore you.

- What does restoration look like in your life?

AFTER SESSION ASSIGNMENT

Reflect on the things we discussed in session and review the questions below this week. Journal your thoughts and bring them back to our next counseling session.

1. Humbling ourselves is submitting to God by trusting that He has purposes in our sufferings. How are you not currently trusting in God?

2. What did you learn about pride and humility and how that relates to your suffering?

3. What definitions of the commands above stood out to you the most and why?

4. Read Psalms 37:5; 40:17; and 55:12; and Matthew 6:25. What do you learn about your cares in these verses? How are these verses relevant to your life?

5. Read Ephesians 2:1–3; 1 John 2:15–16; and 1 Peter 5:8. What do you learn about spiritual warfare and how that relates to your suffering?

Quick Reference Guide

This is a quick reference guide by category. The Scriptures will cover a variety of topics but we hope this will be helpful as you get started.

Anxiety	Luke 6:46–49
Belief	John 11:1–44
Betrayal	John 13:1–5
Compassion	John 7:53–8:11
Conflict	Acts 15:36–41, Philippians 2:1–8
Faith	Mark 4:35–41, Mark 5:25–34, Luke 17:11–19
Forgiveness	John 7:53–8:11
Freedom	Galatians 5:1–4
Grace	James 4
Healing	Mark 1:40–42, John 7:53–8:11, Luke 17:11–19
Heart	Luke 19:1–10, Ephesians 4:31–32
Hope	John 10:22–30, John 11:1–44, Luke 6:46–49, Luke 17:11–19, Hebrews 6:17–20, Hebrews 12:1–3
Humility	John 13:1–5
Identity	John 4:1–30, John 15:1–11, 2 Corinthians 5:16–17
Idolatry	John 15:1–11, John 10:22–30, Acts 17:16–34
Marriage	Philippians 2:1–8, Hebrews 3:12–13
Obedience	Luke 6:46–49
Parenting	Matthew 21:28–32
Pride	James 4
Reconciliation	Acts 15:36–41
Refuge	Hebrews 6:17–20

Relationships	Acts 15:36–41, Ephesians 4:31–32, Philippians 2:1–8, Hebrews 3:12–13, Hebrews 12:1–2
Repentance	Luke 19:1–10, John 4:1–30
Restoration	John 11:1–44
Sin	Ephesians 4:31–32, Hebrews 12:1–3, Hebrews 12:1–2, Rom 6:12–14 & 2 Timothy 2:22
Sorrow	Hebrews 5:7
Spiritual Warfare	Matthew 16:21–23, 1 Peter 5:5–10
Suffering	Matthew 5:2–12, Mark 1:40–42, John 10:22–30, John 11:1–44, Hebrews 6:17–20, Hebrews 12:1–3, 1 Peter 5:5–10
Trauma	Matthew 26:36–46 and Luke 22:40–46
Trust	John 13:1–5
Women	Mark 5:25–34, John 4:1–30, John 7:53–8:11
Worship	Acts 17:16–34

NOTES

NOTES

NOTES